BLACK LEGACY PRESS™
WWW.BLACKLEGACYPRESS.ORG

# SLAVE NARRATIVES

## VOLUME IX
## MISSISSIPPI NARRATIVES

By
United States.
Work Projects Administration

Copyright © 2024 by BLACKLEGACYPRESS.ORG

All rights reserved. No part of this publication may be reproduced or transmitted in any form or by any means electronic or mechanical, including information storage and retrieval systems without permission in writing from the publisher, except for student research using the appropriate citations.

ISBN: 978-1-63652-216-6

# SLAVE NARRATIVES

A Folk History of Slavery in the United States.
From Interviews with Former Slaves

**UNITED STATES.
WORK PROJECTS ADMINISTRATION**

TYPEWRITTEN RECORDS PREPARED BY
THE FEDERAL WRITERS' PROJECT
1936-1938
ASSEMBLED BY
THE LIBRARY OF CONGRESS PROJECT
WORK PROJECTS ADMINISTRATION
FOR THE DISTRICT OF COLUMBIA
SPONSORED BY THE LIBRARY OF
CONGRESS

WASHINGTON 1941

# VOLUME IX
## MISSISSIPPI NARRATIVES

Prepared by
The Federal Writers' Project of
The Works Progress Administration
For the State of Mississippi

# CONTENTS

Jim Allen ............................................................................. 1
Anna Baker ....................................................................... 11
John Cameron .................................................................. 19
Gus Clark .......................................................................... 23
James Cornelius ............................................................... 27
Charlie Davenport ............................................................ 35
Gabe Emanuel .................................................................. 47
Dora Franks ...................................................................... 53
Pet Franks ........................................................................ 61
Nettie Henry ..................................................................... 67
Fanny Smith Hodges ........................................................ 75
Wayne Holliday ................................................................ 79
Prince Johnson ................................................................. 83
Hamp Kennedy ................................................................. 93
James Lucas ..................................................................... 99
Sam Mcallum .................................................................. 109
Charlie Moses ................................................................. 123
Henri Necaise ................................................................. 129
James Singleton ............................................................. 135
Berry Smith .................................................................... 139
Susan Snow .................................................................... 147
Isaac Stier ...................................................................... 157

Jane Sutton ................................................................................. 165
Mollie Williams ........................................................... 171
Tom Wilson ................................................................. 179
Clara C. Young ........................................................... 185

Mississippi Federal Writers
Slave Autobiographies
Jim Allen, Clay Co.
FEC
Mrs. Ed Joiner

[JIM ALLEN
West Point, Mississippi]

# JIM ALLEN

Jim Allen, West Point, age 87, lives in a shack furnished by the city. With him lives his second wife, a much older woman. Both he and his wife have a reputation for being "queer" and do not welcome outside visitors. However, he readily gave an interview and seemed most willing to relate the story of his life.

"Yas, ma'm, I 'members lots about slav'ry time, 'cause I was old 'nough.

"I was born in Russell County, Alabamy, an' can tell you 'bout my own mammy an' pappy an' sisters an' brudders.

"Mammy's name was Darkis an' her Marster was John Bussey, a reg'lar old drunkard, an' my pappy's name was John Robertson an' b'longed to Dr. Robertson, a big farmer on Tombigbee river, five miles east of Columbus. De doctor hisself lived in Columbus.

"My sister Harriett and brudder John was fine fiel'

hands an' Marster kep' 'em in de fiel' most of de time, tryin' to dodge other white folks.

"Den dere was Sister Vice an' brudder George. Befo' I could 'member much, I 'members Lee King had a saloon close to Bob Allen's store in Russell County, Alabama, and Marse John Bussey drunk my mammy up. I means by dat, Lee King tuk her an' my brudder George fer a whiskey debt. Yes, old Marster drinked dem up. Den dey was car'ied to Florida by Sam Oneal, an' George was jes a baby. You know, de white folks wouldn't often sep'rate de mammy an' baby. I ain't seen' em since.

"Did I work? Yes ma'm, me an' a girl worked in de fiel', carryin' one row; you know, it tuk two chullun to mek one han'.

"Did we have good eatins? Yes ma'm, old Marster fed me so good, fer I was his pet. He never 'lowed no one to pester me neither. Now dis Marster was Bob Allen who had tuk me for a whiskey debt, too. Marse Bussey couldn't pay, an' so Marse Allen tuk me, a little boy, out'n de yard whar I was playin' marbles. De law 'lowed de fust thing de man saw, he could take.

"I served Marse Bob Allen 'til Gen'al Grant come 'long and had me an' some others to follow him to Miss'sippi. We was in de woods hidin' de mules an' a fine mare. Dis was after Emanc'pation, an' Gen'al Grant was comin' to Miss'sippi to tell de niggers dey was free.

"As I done tol' you, I was Marse Allen's pet nigger boy. I was called a stray. I slep' on de flo' by old Miss an' Marse Bob. I could'a slep' on de trun'le bed, but it was so easy jes to roll over an' blow dem ashes an' mek dat fire burn.

"Ole Miss was so good, I'd do anything fer her. She was so good an' weighed' round 200 poun's. She was Marse Bob's secon' wife. Nobody 'posed on me, No, Sir! I car'ied water to Marse Bob's sto' close by an' he would allus give me candy by de double han'full, an' as many juice harps as I wanted. De bes' thing I ever did eat was dat candy. Marster was good to his only stray nigger.

"Slave niggers didn't fare wid no gardens 'cept de big garden up at de Big House, when fiel' han's was called to wuk out hers (old Miss). All de niggers had a sight of good things to eat from dat garden an' smoke house.

"I kin see old Lady Sally now, cookin' for us niggers, an' Ruth cooked in de white folk's kitchen. Ruth an' old Man Pleas' an' old Lady Susan was give to Marse Bob when he mar'ied an' come to Sandford, Alabamy.

"No, dere wa'nt no jails, but a guard house. When niggers did wrong, dey was oft'n sent dere, but mos' allus dey was jes whupped when too lazy to wuk, an' when dey would steal.

"Our clo'es was all wove and made on de plan'ation. Our ever'day ones, we called 'hick'ry strips.' We had a' plen'y er good uns. We was fitted out an' out each season, an' had two pairs of shoes, an' all de snuff an' 'bacco we wanted every month.

"No, not any weddin's. It was kinder dis way. Dere was a good nigger man an' a good nigger woman, an' the Marster would say, 'I knows you both good niggers an' I wants you to be man an' wife dis year an' raise little niggers; den I won't have to buy' em.'

"Marse Bob lived in a big white house wid six rooms. He had a cou't house an' a block whar he hired out niggers, jes like mules an' cows.

"How many slaves did us have? Les' see. Dere was old Lady Sally an' her six chullun an' old Jake, her husban', de ox driver, fer de boss. Den dere was old Starlin', Rose, his wife an' fo' chullun. Some of dem was mixed blood by de oberseer. I sees 'em right now. I knowed de oberseer was nothin' but po' white trash, jes a tramp. Den dere was me an' Katherin. Old Lady Sally cooked for de oberseers, seven miles 'way frum de Big House.

"Ever'body was woke up at fo' o'clock by a bugle blowed mos'ly by a nigger, an' was at dey work by sunup. Den dey quits at sunset. I sho' seed bad niggers whupped as many times as dere is leaves on dat groun'. Not Marse Bob's niggers, but our neighbors. We was called 'free,' 'cause Marse Bob treated us so good. The whuppin' was done by de oberseer or driver, who would say as he put de whup to de back, 'Pray sir, pray sir!'

"I seed slaves sol' oft'ener dan you got fingers an' toes. You know I tol' you dere was a sellin' block close to our sto'. Den plen'y niggers had to be chained to a tree or post 'cause he would run 'way an' wouldn' wuk.

"Dey would track de runways wid dogs an' sometimes a white scal'wag or slacker wud be kotched dodgin' duty. I seed as many deserters as I see corn stalks ober in dat fiel'. Dey would hide out in day time an' steal at night.

"No'm I didn' learn to read an' write but my folks

teached me to be honest an' min' Old Miss an' Granny. Dey didn' want us to learn how to go to de free country.

"We had a neighborhood chu'ch an bofe black an' white went to it. Dere was a white preacher an' sometimes a nigger preacher would sit in de pulpit wid him. De slaves set on one side of de aisle an' white folks on de other. I allus liked preacher Williams Odem, an' his brudder Daniel, de 'Slidin' Elder'.[FN: back slider] Dey come frum Ohio. Marse Bob Allen was head steward. I' members lots of my fav'rite songs. Some of dem was, Am I born to Die, Alas and Did my Savior Bleed, an' Must I to de Judgment be Brought. The preacher would say 'Pull down de line and let de spirit be a witnes, workin' fer faith in de future frum on high.'

"I seed de patyrollers every week. If de niggers didn' get a pass in han' right frum one plan'ation to 'nother, dem patyrollers would git you. Dey would be six an' twelve in a drove, an' day would git you if you didn' have dat piece of paper. No sun could go down on a pass. Dere was no trouble twixt niggers den.

"We lay down an' res' at night in de week time. Niggers in slav'ry time riz up in de Quarters, you could hear 'em for miles. Den da cornshucking tuk place. Den we would have singin'. When one foun' a red ear of corn, dey would take a drink of whiskey frum de jug an' cup. We'd get through' bout ten o'clock. De men did'n care if dey worked all night, fer we had the 'Heav'nly Banners'[FN: women and whiskey] by us[HW:?].

"Sometimes we worked on Sat'day a'ternoon, owin' to de crops; but women all knocked off on Sat'day a'ternoon. On Sat'day night, we mos'ly had fun, playin' an drinking whiskey an' beer—no time to fool 'roun' in de week time.

"Some went to chu'ch an' some went fishin' on Sunday. On Chris'mas we had a time—all kinds eatin'—wimmen got new dresses—men tobacco—had stuff to las' 'til Summer. Niggers had good times in mos' ways in slav'ry time. July 4th, we would wash up an' have a good time. We hallowed dat day wid de white folks. Dere was a barbecue; big table set down in bottoms. Dere was niggers strollin' 'roun' like ants. We was havin' a time now. White folks too. When a slave died, dere was a to-do over dat, hollerin' an' singin'. More fuss dan a little—'Well, sich a one has passed out an we gwine to de grave to 'tend de fun'ral; we will talk about Sister Sallie.' De niggers would be jumpin' as high as a cow er mule.

"A song we used to sing was"

**[HW: Sang]**

'Come on Chariot an' Take Her Home, Take Her Home,
Here Come Chariot, les' ride,
Come on les' ride, Come on les' ride.'

"Yessum we believed ha'nts would be at de grave yard. I didn' pay no' tention to dem tho', for I know de evil spirit is dere. Iffen you don't believe it, let one of 'em slap you. I ain't seed one, but I'se heard 'em. I seed someone, dey said was a ghos', but it got 'way quick.

"When we got sick de doctor come at once, and Mistiss was right dere to see we was cared fer. A doctor lived on our place. If you grunt he was right dere. We had castor oil an' pills an' turpentine an' quinine when needful, an' herbs was used. I can fin' dat stuff now what we used when I was a boy.

## [HW: Superstition]

"Some of us wore brass rings on our fingers to keep off croup. Really good—good now. See mine?

"Yessum I knows all 'bout when Yankees come. Dey got us out'er de swamp. I was layin' down by a white oak tree 'sleep, an' when I woke up an' looked up an' saw nothin' but blue, blue, I said, 'Yonder is my Boss's fine male hoss, Alfred. He 'tended dat horse hisself.' He took it to heart, an' he didn' live long afte' de Blue Coats took Alfred.

"Peace was declared to us fust in January in Alabamy, but not in Miss'sippi 'til Grant come back, May 8th.

"I ain't seen my boss since dem Yankees took me 'way. I was seven miles down in de swamp when I was tuk. I wouldn' of tol' him goodbye. I jes wouldn' of lef' him. No sir, I couldn' have lef' my good boss. He tol' me dem Yankees was comin' to take me off. I never wanted to see him 'cause I would have went back 'cause he pertected me an' loved me.

"Like dis week, I lef' de crowd. One day, Cap'in Bob McDaniel came by, an' asked me if I wanted to mek fires an' wuk 'round de house. I said, 'I'd like to see de town whar you want me to go, an' den I come to West Point. It wa'nt nothin' but cotton rows—lot of old shabby shanties, with jes one brick sto', an' it b'longed to Ben Robertson, an' I hope[FN: helped] build all de sto'es in West Point since den.

"I seed de KuKlux. We would be workin'. Dem people would be in de fiel', an' must get home 'fo dark an' shet de door. Dey wo' three cornered white hats with de eyes way up high. Dey skeered de breeches off'n me. First ones I got tangled up wid was right down here by de cemetery. Dey just wanted to scare you. Night riders was de same thing. I was one of de fellers what broke 'em up.

"Old man Toleson was de head leader of de Negroes. Tryin' to get Negroes to go 'gainst our white people. I spec' he was a two faced Yankee or carpetbagger.

"We had clubs all 'round West Point. Cap'in Shattuck out about Palo Alto said to us niggers one day, 'Stop your foolishness—go live among your white folks an' behave. Have sense an' be good citizens.' His advice was good an' we soon broke up our clubs.

"I ain't been to no school 'cept Sunday School since Surrender. A good white man I worked with taught me 'nough to spell 'comprestibility' and 'compastibility.' I had good 'membrance an' I could have learned what white folks taught me, an' dey sees dey manners in me.

"I mar'ied when I was turnin' 19, an' my wife, 15. I mar'ied at big Methodist Chu'ch in Needmore. Same old chu'ch is dere now. I hope build it in 1865. Aunt Emaline Robertson an' Vincent Petty an' Van McCanley started a school in de northeast part of town two years afte' de War.

"Emaline was Mr. Ben Robertson's cook, an' her darter, Callie, was his housekeeper, an' George an' Walter was mechanics. George became a school teacher.

"Abraham Lincoln worked by 'pinions of de Bible.

He got his meanin's from de Bible. 'Every man should live under his own vine and fig tree.' Dis was Abraham's commandments. Dis is where Lincoln started, 'no one should work for another.'

"Jefferson Davis wanted po' man to work for rich man. He was wrong in one 'pinion, an' right in t'other. He tried to take care of his Nation. In one instance, Lincoln was destroying us.

"I j'ined the church to do better an' to be with Christians an' serve Christ. Dis I learned by 'sociation an' harmonious livin' with black an' white, old an' young, an' to give justice to all.

"Be fust work I did after de War was for Mr. Bob McDaniel who lived near Waverly on de Tombigbee River. Yes ma'am, I knowed de Lees, an' de Joiners, but on de river den an' long afte', an' worked for 'em lots in Clay County."

United States. Work Projects Administration

**Anna Baker, Ex-slave, Monroe County**
**FEC**
**Mrs. Richard Kolb**
**Rewrite, Pauline Loveless**
**Edited, Clara E. Stokes**

**ANNA BAKER**
**Aberdeen, Mississippi**

# ANNA BAKER

Anna Baker, 80-year old ex-slave, is tall and well built. She is what the Negroes term a "high brown." Her high forehead and prominent cheek bones indicate that there is a strain of other than the pure African in her blood. She is in fair health.

"Lemme see how old I is. Well, I tells you jus' lak I tol' dat Home Loan man what was here las' week. I 'members a pow'ful lot 'bout slavery times an' 'bout 'fore surrender. I know I was a right smart size den, so's 'cording to dat I mus' be 'roun' 'bout eighty year old. I aint sho' 'bout dat an' I don't want to tell no untruth. I know I was right smart size 'fore de surrender, as I was a-sayin', 'cause I 'members Marster comin' down de road past de house. When I'd see 'im 'way off I'd run to de gate an' start singin' dis song to 'im:

'Here come de marster, root toot too!
Here come Marster, comin' my way!
Howdy, Marster, howdy do!
What you gwine a-bring from town today?'

Dat would mos' nigh tickle him to death an' he'd say, 'Loosahna (dat was his pet name for me) what you want today?' I'd say, 'Bring me some goobers, or a doll, or some stick candy, or anything. An' you can bet yo' bottom doller he'd always bring me somp'n'.

"One reason Marse Morgan thought so much o' me, dey say I was a right peart young'n' an' caught on to anything pretty quick. Marster would tell me, 'Loosanna, if you keep yo' ears open an' tell me what de darkies talk 'bout, dey'll be somp'n' good in it for you.' (He meant for me to listen when dey'd talk 'bout runnin' off an' such.) I'd stay 'roun' de old folks an' make lak I was a-playin'. All de time I'd be a-listenin'. Den I'd go an' tell Marster what I hear'd. But all de time I mus' a-had a right smart mind, 'cause I'd play 'roun' de white folks an' hear what dey'd say an' den go tell de Niggers.—Don't guess de marster ever thought 'bout me doin' dat.

"I was born an' bred 'bout seven miles from Tuscaloosa, Alabama. I was de baby of de fam'ly. De house was on de right han' side o' de road to town. I had four sisters an' one brother dat I knows of. Dey was named Classie, Jennie, Florence, Allie, an' George. My name was Joanna, but dey done drap de Jo part a long time ago.

"I don't recollec' what my ma's mammy an' pappy was named, but I know dat her pappy was a full blooded Injun. (I guess dat is where I gits my brown color.) Her mammy was a full blooded African though, a great big woman.

"I recollec' a tale ray mammy tol' me 'bout my gran'pa. When he took up wid my gran'mammy de white man what owned her say, 'If you want to stay wid her I'll give you a home if you'll work for me lak de Niggers do.' He 'greed, 'cause he thought a heap o' his Black Woman. (Dat's what he called her.) Ever'thing was all right 'til one o' dem uppity overseers tried to act smart. He say he gwine a-beat him. My gran'pappy went home dat night an' barred de door. When de overseer an' some o' his frien's come after him, he say he aint gwine a-open dat door. Dey say if he don't dey gwine a-break it in. He tell' em to go 'head.

"Whilst dey was a-breakin' in he filled a shovel full o' red hot coals an' when dey come in he th'owed it at 'em. Den whilst dey was a-hollerin' he run away. He aint never been seen again to dis good day. I'se hear'd since den dat white folks learnt dat if dey started to whip a Injun dey'd better kill him right den or else he might git dem.

"My mammy's name was Harriet Clemens. When I was too little to know anything 'bout it she run off an' lef' us. I don't 'member much 'bout her 'fore she run off, I reckon I was mos' too little.

"She tol' me when she come after us, after de war was over, all 'bout why she had to run away: It was on 'count of de Nigger overseers. (Dey had Niggers over de hoers an' white mens over de plow han's.) Dey kep' a-tryin' to mess 'roun' wid her an' she wouldn' have nothin' to do wid 'em. One time while she was in de fiel' de overseer asked her to go over to de woods wid him an' she said, 'All right, I'll go find a nice place an' wait.' She jus' kep' a-goin. She swum de river an' run away. She slipped back onct or twict at night to see us, but dat was all. She hired out to some folks dat warnt rich' nough to have no' slaves o' dey own. Dey was good to her, too. (She never lacked for work to do.)

"When my ma went off a old woman called Aunt Emmaline kep' me. (She kep' all de orphunt chillun an' dem who's mammas had been sent off to de breedin' quarters. When dem women had chillun dey brung 'em an' let somebody lak Aunt Emmaline raise em.) She was sho' mean to me. I think it was 'cause de marster laked me an' was always a-pettin' me. She was jealous.

"She was always a-tryin' to whip me for somethin' or nother. One time she hit me wid a iron miggin. (You uses it in churnin'.) It made a bad place on my head. She done it 'cause I let some meal dat she was parchin' burn up. After she done it she got sort a scared an' doctored me up. She put soot on de cut to make it stop bleedin'. Nex' day she made me promise to tell de marster dat I hurt my head when I fell out o' de door dat night he whip Uncle Sim for stealin' a hog. Now I was asleep dat night, but when he asked me I said, 'Aunt Emmaline say tell you I hurt my head fallin' out de door de night you whip Uncle Sim.' Den he say, 'Is dat de truf?' I say, 'Naw sir.' He took Aunt Emmaline down to de gear house an' wore her out. He wouldn' tell off on me. He jus' tol' her dat she had no bus'ness a-lettin' me stay up so late dat I seen him do de whippin'.

"My pa was named George Clemens. Us was all owned by Marster Morgan Clemens. Master Hardy, his daddy, had give us to him when he 'vided out wid de res' o' his chillun. (Marster Morgan was a settled man. He went 'roun' by hisse'f mos' o' de time. He never did marry.)

"My pa went to de war wid Marster Morgan an' he never come back. I don't 'member much 'bout 'em goin', but after dey lef' I 'member de Blue Coats a-comin'. Dey tore de smoke house down an' made a big fire an' cooked all de meat dey could hol'. All us Niggers had a good time, 'cause, dey give us all us wanted. One of 'em put me up on his knee an' asked me if I'd ever seen Marster wid any little bright 'roun' shiny things. (He held his hand up wid his fingers in de shape of a dollar.) I, lak a crazy little Nigger said, 'Sho', Marster draps 'em 'hind de mantelpiece.' Den, if dey didn' tear dat mantel down an' git his money, I's a son-of-a-gun!

"After de war was over my ma got some papers from de progo[FN: provost] marshal. She come to de place an 'tol' de marster she want her chillun. He say she can have all 'cept me. She say she want me, too, dat I was her'n an' she was gwine a-git me. She went back an 'got some more papers an' showed 'em to Marster Morgan. Den he lemme go.

"She come out to de house to git us. At firs' I was scared o' her, 'cause I didn' know who she was. She put me in her lap an' she mos' nigh cried when she seen de back o' my head. Dey was awful sores where de lice had been an' I had scratched 'em. (She sho' jumped Aunt Emmaline 'bout dat.) Us lef' dat day an' went right on to Tuscaloosa. My ma had married again an' she an' him took turns 'bout carrying me when I got tired. Us had to walk de whole seven miles.

"I went to school after dat an' learnt to read an' write. Us had white Yankee teachers. I learnt to read de Bible well' nough an' den I quit.

"I was buried in de water lak de Savior. I's a real Baptis'. De Holy Sperrit sho' come into my heart.

"I b'lieves in de Sperrit. I b'lieves all o' us when us

dies is sperrits. Us jus' hovers 'roun' in de sky a-ridin' on de clouds. Course, some folks is born wid a cloud over dey faces. Dey can see things dat us can't. I reckon dey sees de sperrits. I know' bout dem Kloo Kluxes. I had to go to court one time to testify 'bout' em. One night after us had moved to Tuscaloosa dey come after my step-daddy. Whilst my ma an' de res' went an' hid I went to de door. I warnt scared. I says, 'Marster Will, aint dat you?' He say, 'Sho', it's me. Whar's yo' daddy?' I tol' 'im dat he'd gone to town. Den dey head out for 'im. In de meantime my ma she had started out, too. She warned him to hide, so dey didn' git 'im.

"Soon after dat de Yankees hel' a trial in Tuscaloosa. Dey carried me. A man hel' me up an' made me p'int out who it was dat come to our house. I say, 'Dat's de man, aint it Marster Will?' He couldn' say "No", 'cause he'd tol' me twas him dat night. Dey put 'em in jail for six months an' give 'em a big fine.

"Us moved from Tuscaloosa while I was still a young girl an' went to Pickensville, Alabama. Us stayed dar on de river for awhile an' den moved to Columbus, Mississippi. I lived dar 'til I was old 'nough to git out to myse'f.

"Den I come to Aberdeen an' married Sam Baker. Me an' Sam done well. He made good money an' us bought dis very house I lives in now. Us never had no chillun, but I was lef' one by a cousin o' mine what died. I raised her lak she was my own. I sont her to school an' ever'thing. She lives in Chicago now an' wants me to come live wid her. But shucks! What would a old woman lak me do in a place lak dat?

"I aint got nothin' lef now 'cept a roof over my head.

I wouldn' have dat 'cept for de President o' de United States. Dey had loaned me some money to fix up de house to keep it from fallin' down on me. Dey said I'd have fifteen year to pay it back in. Now course, I knowed I'd be dead in dat time, so I signed up wid' em.

"Las' year de men dat collec' nearly worrit me to death a-tryin' to git some money from me. I didn' have none, so dey say dey gwine a-take my home.

"Now I hear tell o' dat barefoot Nigger down at Columbus callin' de president an' him bein' so good to 'im. So I 'cided to write an' tell 'im what a plight dis Nigger was in. I didn' say nothin noxious[FN: obnoxious], but I jus' tol' him plain facts. He writ me right back an' pretty soon he sont a man down to see me. He say I needn' bother no more, dat dey won't take my house 'way from me. An' please de Lawd! Dey aint nobody else been here a-pesterin' me since.

"Dat man tol' me soon as de old age pension went th'ough I'd git thirty dollars a mont' stid[FN: instead] o' de four I's a-gittin' now. Now won't dat be gran'? I could live lak de white folks on dat much.

"I'se had 'ligion all my born days. (I never learnt to read de Bible an' 'terpet de Word 'til I was right smart size, but I mus' o' b'lieved in de Lawd since 'way back.) I'se gwine a-go right 'long an' keep a-trustin' de good Lawd an' I knows ever'thing gwine a-come out all right.

"'Twixt de Lawd an' de good white folks I know I's gwine always have somethin' t'eat. President Roosevelt done 'tended to de roof over my head."

United States. Work Projects Administration

**JOHN CAMERON**
Jackson, Mississippi

# JOHN CAMERON

John Cameron, ex-slave, lives in Jackson. He was born in 1842 and was owned by Howell Magee. He is five feet six inches tall, and weighs about 150 pounds. His general coloring is blackish-brown with white kinky hair. He is in fairly good health.

"I'se always lived right here in Hinds County. I's seen Jackson grow from de groun' up.

"My old Marster was de bes' man in de worl'. I jus' wish I could tell, an' make it plain, jus' how good him an' old Mistis was. Marster was a rich man. He owned 'bout a thousand an' five hund'ed acres o' lan' an' roun' a hund'ed slaves. Marster's big two-story white house wid lightning rods standin' all 'bout on de roof set on top of a hill.

"De slave cabins, 'cross a valley from de Big House, was built in rows. Us was 'lowed to sing, play de fiddles, an' have a good time. Us had plenty t' eat and warm clo'es an' shoes in de winter time. De cabins was kep' in good shape. Us aint never min' workin' for old Marster, cause us got good returns. Dat meant good livin' an' bein' took care of right. Marster always fed his slaves in de Big House.

"De slaves would go early to de fiel's an work in de cotton an' corn. Dey had different jobs.

"De overseers was made to un'erstan' to be 'siderate of us. Work went on all de week lak dat. Dey got off from de fiel's early on Satu'd'y evenin's, washed up an' done what dey wanted to. Some went huntin' or fishin', some fiddled an' danced an' sung, while de others jus' lazed roun' de cabins. Marse had two of de slaves jus' to be fiddlers. Dey played for us an' kep' things perked up. How us could swing, an' step-'bout by dat old fiddle music always a-goin' on. Den old Marster come 'roun' wid his kin'ly smile an' jov'al sp'rits. When things went wrong he always knowed a way. He knowed how to comfort you in trouble.

"Now, I was a gardner or yard boy. Dat was my part as a slave. I he'ped keep de yard pretty an' clean, de grass cut, an' de flowers' tended to an' cut. I taken dat work' cause I lak's pretty flowers. I laks to buil' frames for 'em to run on an' to train 'em to win' 'roun'. I could monkey wid 'em all de time.

"When folks started a-comin' through talkin' 'bout a-freein' us an' a-givin' us lan' an' stuff, it didn' take wid Marster's slaves. Us didn' want nothin' to come 'long to take us away from him. Dem a tellin' de Niggers dey'd git lan' an' cattle an' de lak of dat was all foolis'ness, nohow. Us was a-livin' in plenty an' peace.

"De war broke out spite o' how Marster's Niggers felt. When I seen my white folks leave for war, I cried myself sick, an' all de res' did too. Den de Yankees come through a-takin' de country. Old Marster refugeed us to Virginny. I can't say if de lan' was his'n, but he had a place for us to stay at. I know us raised 'nough food stuff for all de slaves. Marster took care o' us dere 'til de war ended.

"Den he come to camp late one evenin' an tol' us dat us was free as he was; dat us could stay in Virginny an work or us could come to Mississippi wid him. Might nigh de whole passel bun'led up an' come back, an' glad to do it, too. Dar us all stayed 'til de family all died. De las' one died a few years ago an' lef' us few old darkies to grieve over 'em.

"I don' know much 'bout de Klu Klux Klan an' all dat. Dey rode 'bout at night an' wore long white ghos'-lak robes. Dey whup folks an' had meetin's way off in de woods at midnight. Dey done all kinds o' curious things. None never did bother 'bout Marster's place, so I don' know much 'bout 'em.

"After de War it took a mighty long time to git things a-goin' smooth. Folks an' de Gov'ment, too, seem lak dey was all up-set an' threatened lak. For a long time it look lak things gwine bus' loose ag'in. Mos' ever'thing was tore up an' burned down to de groun'. It took a long time to build back dout no money. Den twant de gran' old place it was de firs' time.

"I married when I was a young man. I was lucky 'nough to git de nex' bes' woman in de worl'. (Old Mis' was de bes'.) Dat gal was so good 'til I had to court 'er mos' two years 'fore she'd say she'd have me.

"Us had six chillun. Three of 'em's still livin'. I can't say much for my chillun. I don' lak to feel hard, but I tried to raise my chillun de bes' I could. I educated 'em; even bought 'em a piano an' give em' music. One of 'em is in

Memphis, 'nother'n in Detroit, an' de other'n in Chicago. I writes to 'em to he'p me, but don' never hear from 'em. I's old an' dey is forgot me, I guess.

"Dat seems to be de way of de worl' now. Ever'thing an' ever'body is too fas' an' too frivoless[FN: frivilous] dese here times. I tell you, folks ought to be more lak old Marster was.

"I's a Christian an' loves de Lawd. I expects to go to him 'fore long. Den I know I's gwine see my old Marstar an' Mistis ag'in."

## BIBLIOGRAPHY

John Cameron: Jackson, Mississippi.

**Mississippi Federal Writers
Slave Autobiographies**

[GUS CLARK
Howison, Mississippi]

# GUS CLARK

Uncle Gus Clark and his aged wife live in a poverty-stricken deserted village about an eighth of a mile east of Howison.

Their old mill cabin, a relic of a forgotten lumber industry, is tumbling down. They received direct relief from the ERA until May, 1934, when the ERA changed the dole to work relief. Uncle Gus, determined to have a work card, worked on the road with the others until he broke down a few days later and was forced to accept direct relief. Now, neither Gus nor Liza is able to work, and the only help available for them is the meager State Old Age Assistance. Gus still manages to tend their tiny garden.

He gives his story:

"I'se gwine on 'bout eighty-five. 'At's my age now. I was born at Richmond, Virginny, but lef' dare right afte' de War. Dey had done surrendered den, an' my old marster doan have no mo' power over us. We was all free an' Boss turned us loose.

"My mammy's name was Judy, an' my pappy was Bob. Clark was de Boss's name. I doan 'member my mammy, but pappy was workin' on de railroad afte' freedom an' got killed.

"A man come to Richmond an' carried me an' pappy an' a lot of other niggers ter Loos'anna ter work in de sugar cane. I was little but he said I could be a water boy. It sho' was a rough place. Dem niggers quar'l an' fight an' kills one 'nother. Big Boss, he rich, an' doan 'low no sheriff ter come on his place. He hol' cou't an' settle all 'sputes hisself. He done bury de dead niggers an' put de one what killed him back to work.

"A heap of big rattlesnakes lay in dem canebrakes, an' dem niggers shoot dey heads off an' eat 'em. It didn' kill de niggers. Dem snakes was fat an' tender, an' fried jes lak chicken.

"Dere in Loos'anna we doan get no pay 'til de work is laid by. Den we'se paid big money, no nickels. Mos' of de cullud mens go back to where dey was raised.

"Dat was afte' freedom, but my daddy say dat de niggers earn money on Old Boss' place even durin' slav'ry. He give 'em every other Sat'dy fer deyse'ves. Dey cut cordwood fer Boss, wimmens an' all. Mos' of de mens cut two cords a day an' de wimmens one. Boss paid 'em a dollar a cord. Dey save dat money, fer dey doan have to pay it out fer nothin'. Big Boss didn' fail to feed us good an' give us our work clo'es. An' he paid de doctor bills. Some cullud men saved enough to buy deyse'ves frum Boss, as free as I is now.

"Slav'ry was better in some ways 'an things is now. We allus got plen'y ter eat, which we doan now. We can't make but fo' bits a day workin' out now, an' 'at doan buy nothin' at de sto'. Co'se Boss only give us work clo'es. When I was a kid I got two os'berg[FN: Osnaberg: the cheapest grade of cotton cloth] shirts a year. I never wo' no shoes. I didn' know whut a shoe was made fer, 'til I'se twelve or thirteen. We'd go rabbit huntin' barefoot in de snow.

"Didn' wear no Sunday clo'es. Dey wa'nt made fer me, 'cause I had nowhere ter go. You better not let Boss ketch you off'n de place, less'n he give you a pass to go. My Boss didn' 'low us to go to church, er to pray er sing. Iffen he ketched us prayin' er singin' he whupped us. He better not ketch you with a book in yo' han'. Didn' 'low it. I doan know whut de reason was. Jess meanness, I reckin. I doan b'lieve my marster ever went to church in his life, but he wa'nt mean to his niggers, 'cept fer doin' things he doan 'low us to. He didn' care fer nothin' 'cept farmin'.

"Dere wa'nt no schools fer cullud people den. We didn' know whut a school was. I never did learn to read.

"We didn' have no mattresses on our beds like we has now. De chullun slep' under de big high beds, on sacks. We was put under dem beds 'bout eight o'clock, an' we'd jes better not say nothin' er make no noise afte' den. All de cullud folks slep' on croker sacks full of hay er straw.

"Did I ever see any niggers punished? Yessum, I sho' has. Whupped an' chained too. Day was whupped 'til de blood come, 'til dey back split all to pieces. Den it was washed off wid salt, an' de nigger was put right back in de fiel'. Dey was whupped fer runnin' away. Sometimes dey run afte' 'em fer days an nights with dem big old blood houn's. Heap o' people doan b'lieve dis. But I does, 'cause I seed it myse'f.

"I'se lived here forty-five years, an' chipped turpentine mos' all my life since I was free.

"I'se had three wives. I didn' have no weddin's, but I mar'ied 'em 'cordin to law. I woan stay with one no other way. My fust two wives is dead. Liza an' me has been mar'ied 'bout 'leven years. I never had but one chile, an' 'at by my fust wife, an' he's dead. But my other two wives had been mar'ied befo', an' had chullun. 'Simon here,' pointing to a big buck of fifty-five sitting on the front porch, 'is Liza's oldest boy.'"

**Mississippi Federal Writers**
**Slave Autobiographies**

[JAMES CORNELIUS
Magnolia, Mississippi]

# JAMES CORNELIUS

James Cornelius lives in Magnolia in the northwestern part of the town, in the Negro settlement. He draws a Confederate pension of four dollars per month. He relates events of his life readily.

"I does not know de year I was borned but dey said I was 15 years old when de War broke out an' dey tell me I'se past 90 now. Dey call me James Cornelius an' all de white folks says I'se a good 'spectable darkey.

"I was borned in Franklin, Loos'anna. My mammy was named Chlo an' dey said my pappy was named Henry. Dey b'longed to Mr. Alex Johnson an' whil'st I was a baby my mammy, my brudder Henry, an' me was sol' to Marse Sam Murry Sandell an' we has brung to Magnolia to live an' I niver remember seein' my pappy ag'in.

"Marse Murry didn' have many slaves. His place was right whar young Mister Lampton Reid is buildin' his fine house jes east of de town. My mammy had to work in da house an' in de fiel' wid all de other niggers an' I played in de yard wid de little chulluns, bofe white an' black. Sometimes we played 'tossin' de ball' an' sometimes we played 'rap-jacket' an' sometimes 'ketcher.' An' when it rained we had to go in de house an' Old Mistess made us behave.

"I was taught how to work 'round de house, how to sweep an' draw water frum de well an' how to kin'le fires an' keep de wood box filled wid wood, but I was crazy to larn how to plow an' when I could I would slip off an' get a old black man to let me walk by his side an' hold de lines an' I thought I was big 'nouf to plow.

"Marse Murry didn' have no overseer. He made de slaves work, an' he was good an' kind to 'em, but when dey didn' do right he would whip 'em, but he didn' beat 'em. He niver stripped 'em to whip 'em. Yes ma'm, he whipped me but I needed it. One day I tol' him I was not goin' to do whut he tol' me to do—feed de mule—but when he got through wid me I wanted to feed dat mule.

"I come to live wid Marse Murry 'fo dar was a town here. Dar was only fo' houses in dis place when I was a boy. I seed de fust train dat come to dis here town an' it made so much noise dat I run frum it. Dat smoke puffed out'n de top an' de bell was ringin' an' all de racket it did make made me skeered.

"I heered dem talkin' 'bout de war but I didn' know whut dey meant an' one day Marse Murry said he had jined de Quitman Guards an' was goin' to de war an' I had to go wid him. Old Missus cried an' my mammy cried but I thought it would be fun. He tuk me 'long an' I waited on him. I kept his boots shinin' so yer could see yer face in 'em. I brung him water an' fed an' cur'ied his hoss an' put his saddle on de hoss fer him. Old Missus tol' me to be good to him an' I was.

"One day I was standin' by de hoss an' a ball kilt[FN: killed] de hoss an' he fell over dead an' den I cried like it mout[FN: might] be my brudder. I went way up in Tennessee an' den I was at Port Hudson. I seed men fall dawn an' die; dey was kilt like pigs. Marse Murry was shot an' I stayed wid him 'til dey could git him home. Dey lef' me behin' an' Col. Stockdale an' Mr. Sam Matthews brung me home.

"Marse Murry died an' Old Missus run de place. She was good an' kind to us all an' den she mar'ied afte' while to Mr. Gatlin. Dat was afte' de war was over.

"Whil'st I was in de war I seed Mr. Jeff Davis. He was ridin' a big hoss an' he looked mighty fine. I niver seed him 'ceptin he was on de hoss.

"Dey said old man Abe Lincoln was de nigger's friend, but frum de way old Marse an' de sojers talk 'bout him I thought he was a mighty mean man.

"I doan recollec' when dey tol' us we was freed but I do know Mr. Gatlin would promise to pay us fer our work an' when de time would come fer to pay he said he didn' have it an' kep' puttin us off, an' we would work some more an' git nothin' fer it. Old Missus would cry an' she was good to us but dey had no money.

"'Fo de war Marse Murry would wake all de niggers by blowin' a big 'konk' an' den when dinner time would come Old Missus would blow de 'konk' an' call dem to dinner. I got so I could blow dat 'konk' fer Old Missus but oh! it tuk my wind.

"Marse Murry would 'low me to drive his team when he would go to market. I could haul de cotton to Covin'ton an' bring back whut was to eat, an' all de oxen could pull was put on dat wagon. We allus had good eatin afte' we had been to market.

"Every Chris'mus would come I got a apple an' some candy an' mammy would cook cake an' pies fer Old Missus an' stack dem on de shelf in de big kitchen an' we had every thing good to eat. Dem people sho' was good an' kind to all niggers.

"Afte de war de times was hard an' de white an' black people was fightin' over who was to git de big office, an' den dere was mighty leetle to eat. Dar was plen'y whiskey, but I'se kep' 'way frum all dat. I was raised right. Old Missus taught me ter 'spect white folks an' some of dem promised me land but I niver got it. All de land I'se ever got I work mighty hard fer it an' I'se got it yit.

"One day afte' Mr. Gatlin said he couldn' pay me I run 'way an' went to New Orleans an' got a job haulin' cotton, an' made my 50 cents an' dinner every day. I sho' had me plen'y money den. I stayed dere mighty close on to fo' years an' den I went to Tylertown an' hauled cotton to de railroad fer Mr. Ben Lampton. Mr. Lampton said I was de bes' driver of his team he ever had caze I kep' his team fat.

"Afte I come back to Miss'ssippi I mar'ied a woman named Maggie Ransom. We stayed together 51 years. I niver hit her but one time. When we was gittin' mar'ied I stopped de preacher right in de ceremony an' said to her, 'Maggie, iffen you niver call me a liar I will niver call you one' an' she said, 'Jim, I won't call you a liar.' I said, 'That's a bargain' an' den de preacher went on wid de weddin'. Well, one day afte' we had been mar'ied' bout fo' years, she ast[FN: asked] me how come I was so late comin' to supper, an' I said I found some work to do fer a white lady, an' she said, that's a lie,' an' right den I raised my han' an' let her have it right by de side of de head, an' she niver called me a liar ag'in. No ma'm, dat is somethin' I won't stand fer.

"My old lady had seven chulluns dat lived to git grown. Two of 'em lived here in Magnolia an' de others gone North. Maggie is daid an' I live wid my boy Walter an' his wife Lena. Dey is mighty good to me. I owns dis here house an' fo' acres but day live wid me an' I gits a Confed'rate pension of fo' dollars a month. Dat gives me my coffee an' 'bacco. I'se proud I'se a old sojer, I seed de men fall when dey was shot but I was not skeered. We et bread when we could git it an' if we couldn' git it we done widout.

"Afte' I lef' Mr. Lampton I'se come here an' went to work fer Mr. Enoch at Fernwood when his mill was jes a old rattletrap of a mill. I work fer him 45 years. At fust I hauled timber out'n de woods an' afte' whil'st I hauled lumber to town to build houses. I sometimes collec' fer de lumber but I niver lost one nickle, an' dem white folks says I sho' was a honest nigger.

"I lived here on dis spot an' rode a wheel to Fernwood every day, an' fed de teams an' hitched 'em to de wagons an' I was niver late an' niver stopped fer anything, an' my wheel niver was in de shop. I niver 'lowed anybody to prank wid it, an' dat wheel was broke up by my gran'chulluns.

"Afte I quit work at de mill I'se come home an' plow

gardens fer de white folks an' make some more money. I sho' could plow.

"I jined de New Zion Baptist Church here in Magnolia an' was baptized in de Tanghipoa River one Sunday evenin'. I was so happy dat I shouted, me an' my wife bofe. I'se still a member of dat church but I do not preach an' I'm not no deacon; I'se jes a bench member an' a mighty po' one at dat. My wife was buried frum dat church.

"Doan know why I was not called Jim Sandell, but mammy said my pappy was named Henry Cornelius an' I reckin I was give my pappy's name.

"When I was a young man de white folks' Baptist Church was called Salem an' it was on de hill whar de graveyard now is. It burnt down an' den dey brung it to town, an' as I was goin' to tell yer I went possum huntin' in dat graveyard one night. I tuk my ax an' dog 'long wid me an' de dog, he treed a possum right in de graveyard. I cut down dat tree an' started home, when all to once somethin' run by me an' went down dat big road lak light'ning an' my dog was afte' it. Den de dog come back an' lay down at my feet an' rolled on his back an' howled an' howled, an' right den I knowed it was a sperit an' I throwed down my 'possum an' ax an' beat de dog home. I tell you dat was a sperit—I'se seed plen'y of 'em. Dat ain't de only sperit I ever seed. I'se seen 'em a heap of times. Well, dat taught me niver to hunt in a grave yard ag'in.

"No ma'm, I niver seed a ghost but I tell yer I know dere is sperits. Let me tell yer, anudder time I was goin' by de graveyard an' I seed a man's head. He had no feet, but he kep' lookin' afte' me an' every way I turned he wouldn' take his eye offen me, an' I walked fast an' he got faster an' den I run an' den he run, an' when I got home I jes fell on de bed an' hollered an' hollered an' tol' my old lady, an' she said I was jes' skeered, but I'se sho' seed dat sperit an' I ain't goin' by de grave yard at night by myse'f ag'in.

An' let me tell yer dis. Right in front of dis house—yer see dat white house?—Well, last Febr'ary a good old cullud lady died in dat house, an' afte' she was buried de rest of de fambly moved away, an' every night I kin look over to dat house an' see a light in de window. Dat light comes an' goes, an' nobody lives dar. Doan I know dat is de sperit of dat woman comin' back here to tell some of her fambly a message? Yes ma'm, dat is her sperit an' dat house is hanted an' nobody will live dar ag'in.

"No ma'm, I can't read nor write."

United States. Work Projects Administration

Charlie Davenport, Ex-slave, Adams County
FEC
Edith Wyatt Moore
Rewrite, Pauline Loveless
Edited, Clara E. Stokes

[CHARLIE DAVENPORT
Natchez, Mississippi]

# CHARLIE DAVENPORT

"I was named Charlie Davenport an' encordin'[FN: according] to de way I figgers I ought to be nearly a hund'ed years old. Nobody knows my birthday, 'cause all my white folks is gone.

"I was born one night an' de very nex' mornin' my po' little mammy died. Her name was Lucindy. My pa was William Davenport.

"When I was a little mite dey turnt me over to de granny nurse on de plantation. She was de one dat 'tended to de little pickaninnies. She got a woman to nurse me what had a young baby, so I didn' know no dif'ence. Any woman what had a baby 'bout my age would wet nurse me, so I growed up in de quarters an' was as well an' as happy as any other chil'.

"When I could tote taters[FN: sweet potatoes] dey'd let me pick' em up in de fiel'. Us always hid a pile away where us could git' em an' roast' em at night.

"Old mammy nearly always made a heap o' dewberry an' 'simmon[FN: persimmon]. wine.

"Us little tykes would gather black walnuts in de woods an' store 'em under de cabins to dry.

"At night when de work was all done an' de can'les was out us'd set 'roun' de fire an' eat cracked nuts an' taters. Us picked out de nuts wid horse-shoe nails an' baked de taters in ashes. Den Mammy would pour herse'f an' her old man a cup o' wine. Us never got none o' dat less'n[FN: unless] us be's sick. Den she'd mess it up wid wild cherry bark. It was bad den, but us gulped it down, anyhow.

"Old Granny used to sing a song to us what went lak dis:

'Kinky head, whar-fore you skeered?
Old snake crawled off, 'cause he's afeared.
Pappy will smite 'im on de back
Wid a great big club—ker whack! Ker whack!'

"Aventine, where I was born an' bred, was acrost Secon' Creek. It was a big plantation wid 'bout a hund'ed head o' folks a-livin' on it. It was only one o' de marster's places, 'cause he was one o' de riches' an' highes' quality gent'men in de whole country. I's tellin' you de trufe, us didn' b'long to no white trash. De marster was de Honorable Mister Gabriel Shields hisse'f. Ever'body knowed 'bout him. He married a Surget.

"Dem Surgets was pretty devilish; for all dey was de riches' fam'ly in de lan'. Dey was de out-fightin'es', out-cussin'es', fastes' ridin', hardes' drinkin', out-spendin'es' folks I ever seen. But Lawd! Lawd! Dey was gent'men even in dey cups. De ladies was beautiful wid big black eyes an' sof' white han's, but dey was high strung, too.

"De marster had a town mansion what's pictured in a lot o' books. It was called 'Montebella.' De big columns still stan' at de end o' Shields Lane. It burnt 'bout thirty years ago (1937).

"I's part Injun. I aint got no Nigger nose an' my hair is so long I has to keep it wropped[FN: wrapped]. I'se often heard my mammy was redish-lookin' wid long, straight, black hair. Her pa was a full blooded Choctaw an' mighty nigh as young as she was. I'se been tol' dat nobody dast[FN: dared] meddle wid her. She didn' do much talkin', but she sho' was a good worker. My pappy had Injun blood, too, but his hair was kinky.

"De Choctaws lived all 'roun' Secon' Creek. Some of 'em had cabins lak settled folks. I can 'member dey las' chief. He was a tall pow'ful built man named 'Big Sam.' What he said was de law, 'cause he was de boss o' de whole tribe. One rainy night he was kilt in a saloon down in 'Natchez Under de Hill.' De Injuns went wild wid rage an' grief. Dey sung an' wailed an' done a heap o' low mutterin'. De sheriff kep' a steady watch on' em, 'cause he was afeared dey would do somethin' rash. After a long time he kinda let up in his vig'lance. Den one night some o' de Choctaw mens slipped in town an' stobbed[FN: stabbed] de man dey b'lieved had kilt Big Sam. I 'members dat well.

"As I said b'fore, I growed up in de quarters. De houses was clean an' snug. Us was better fed den dan I is now, an' warmer, too. Us had blankets an' quilts filled wid home raised wool an' I jus' loved layin' in de big fat feather bed a-hearin' de rain patter on de roof.

"All de little darkeys he'ped bring in wood. Den us swept de yards wid brush brooms. Den sometimes us played together in de street what run de length o' de quarters. Us th'owed horse-shoes, jumped poles, walked on stilts, an' played marbles. Sometimes us made bows an' arrows. Us could shoot 'em, too, jus lak de little Injuns.

"A heap of times old Granny would brush us hide wid a peach tree limb, but us need it. Us stole aigs[FN: eggs] an' roasted 'em. She sho' wouldn' stan' for no stealin' if she knowed it.

"Us wore lowell-cloth shirts. It was a coarse towsackin'. In winter us had linsey-woolsey pants an' heavy cow-hide shoes. Dey was made in three sizes—big, little, an' mejum[FN: medium]. Twant no right or lef'. Dey was sorta club-shaped so us could wear 'em on either foot.

"I was a teasin', mis-che-vious chil' an' de overseer's little gal got it in for me. He was a big, hard fisted Dutchman bent on gittin' riches. He trained his pasty-faced gal to tattle on us Niggers. She got a heap o' folks whipped. I knowed it, but I was hasty: One day she hit me wid a stick an' I th'owed it back at her. 'Bout dat time up walked her pa. He seen what I done, but he didn' see what she done to me. But it wouldn' a-made no dif'ence, if he had.

"He snatched me in de air an' toted me to a stump an' laid me 'crost it. I didn' have but one thickness 'twixt me an' daylight. Gent'men! He laid it on me wid dat stick. I thought I'd die. All de time his mean little gal was a-gloatin' in my misery. I yelled an' prayed to de Lawd 'til he quit.

"Den he say to me,

'From now on you works in de fiel'. I aint gwine a-have no vicious boy lak you 'roun de lady folks.' I was too little for fiel' work, but de nex' mornin' I went to choppin' cotton. After dat I made a reg'lar fiel' han'. When I growed up I was a ploughman. I could sho' lay off a pretty cotton row, too.

"Us slaves was fed good plain grub. 'Fore us went to de fiel' us had a big breakfas' o' hot bread, 'lasses, fried salt meat dipped in corn meal, an' fried taters[FN: sweet potatoes]. Sometimes us had fish an' rabbit meat. When us was in de fiel', two women 'ud come at dinner-time wid baskets filled wid hot pone, baked taters, corn roasted in de shucks, onion, fried squash, an' b'iled pork. Sometimes dey brought buckets o' cold buttermilk. It sho' was good to a hongry man. At supper-time us had hoecake an' cold vi'tals. Sometimes dey was sweetmilk an' collards.

"Mos' ever' slave had his own little garden patch an' was 'lowed to cook out of it.

"Mos' ever plantation kep' a man busy huntin' an' fishin' all de time. (If dey shot a big buck, us had deer meat roasted on a spit.)

"On Sundays us always had meat pie or fish or fresh game an' roasted taters an' coffee. On Chris'mus de marster 'ud give us chicken an' barrels o' apples an' oranges. 'Course, ever' marster warnt as free handed as our'n was. (He was sho' 'nough quality.) I'se hear'd dat a heap o' cullud people never had nothin' good t'eat.

"I warnt learnt nothin' in no book. Don't think I'd a-took to it, nowhow. Dey learnt de house servants to read. Us fiel' han's never knowed nothin' 'cept weather an' dirt an' to weigh cotton. Us was learnt to figger a little, but dat's all.

"I reckon I was 'bout fifteen when hones' Abe Lincoln what called hisse'f a rail-splitter come here to talk wid us. He went all th'ough de country jus' a-rantin' an' a-preachin' 'bout us bein' his black brothers. De marster didn' know nothin' 'bout it, 'cause it was sorta secret-lak. It sho' riled de Niggers up an' lots of 'em run away. I sho' hear'd him, but I didn' pay 'im no min'.

"When de war broke out dat old Yankee Dutch overseer o' our'n went back up North, where he b'longed. Us was pow'ful glad an' hoped he'd git his neck broke.

"After dat de Yankees come a-swoopin' down on us. My own pappy took off wid 'em. He j'ined a comp'ny what fit[FN: fought] at Vicksburg. I was plenty big 'nough to fight, but I didn' hanker to tote no gun. I stayed on de plantation an' put in a crop.

"It was pow'ful on easy times after dat. But what I care 'bout freedom? Folks what was free was in misery firs' one way an' den de other.

"I was on de plantation closer to town, den. It was called 'Fish Pond Plantation.' De white folks come an' tol' us we mus' burn all de cotton so de enemy couldn' git it.

"Us piled it high in de fiel's lak great mountains. It made my innards hurt to see fire 'tached to somethin' dat had cost us Niggers so much labor an' hones' sweat. If I could a-hid some o' it in de barn I'd a-done it, but de boss searched ever'where.

"De little Niggers thought it was fun. Dey laughed an' brung out big armfuls from de cotton house. One little black gal clapped her han's an' jumped in a big heap. She sunk down an' down' til she was buried deep. Den de wind picked up de flame an' spread it lak lightenin'. It spread so fas' dat 'fore us could bat de eye, she was in a mountain of fiah. She struggled up all covered wid flames, a-screamin',' Lawdy, he'p me!' Us snatched her out an' rolled her on de groun', but twant no use. She died in a few minutes.

"De marster's sons went to war. De one what us loved bes' never come back no more. Us mourned him a-plenty, 'cause he was so jolly an' happy-lak, an' free wid his change. Us all felt cheered when he come 'roun'.

"Us Niggers didn' know nothin' 'bout what was gwine on in de outside worl'. All us knowed was dat a war was bein' fit. Pussonally, I b'lieve in what Marse Jefferson Davis done. He done de only thing a gent'man could a-done. He tol' Marse Abe Lincoln to 'tend to his own bus'ness an' he'd 'tend to his'n. But Marse Lincoln was a fightin' man an' he come down here an' tried to run other folks' plantations. Dat made Marse Davis so all fired mad dat he spit hard 'twixt his teeth an' say, 'I'll whip de socks off dem dam Yankees.'

"Dat's how it all come 'bout.

"My white folks los' money, cattle, slaves, an' cotton in de war, but dey was still better off dan mos' folks.

"Lak all de fool Niggers o' dat time I was right smart bit by de freedom bug for awhile. It sounded pow'ful nice to be tol':

'You don't have to chop cotton no more. You can th'ow dat hoe down an' go fishin' whensoever de notion strikes you. An' you can roam' roun' at night an' court gals jus' as late as you please. Aint no marster gwine a-say to you, "Charlie, you's got to be back when de clock strikes nine."'

"I was fool 'nough to b'lieve all dat kin' o' stuff. But to tell de hones' truf, mos' o' us didn' know ourse'fs no better off. Freedom meant us could leave where us'd been born an' bred, but it meant, too, dat us had to scratch for us ownse'fs. Dem what lef' de old plantation seemed so all fired glad to git back dat I made up my min' to stay put. I stayed right wid my white folks as long as I could.

"My white folks talked plain to me. Dey say real sadlak, 'Charlie, you's been a dependence, but now you can go if you is so desirous. But if you wants to stay wid us you can share-crop. Dey's a house for you an' wood to keep you warm an' a mule to work. We aint got much cash, but dey's de lan' an' you can count on havin' plenty o' vit'als. Do jus' as you please.' When I looked at my marster an' knowed he needed me, I pleased to stay. My marster never forced me to do nary thing' bout it. Didn' nobody make me work after de war, but dem Yankees sho' made my daddy work. Dey put a pick in his han' stid[FN: instead] o' a gun. Dey made' im dig a big ditch in front o' Vicksburg.

He worked a heap harder for his Uncle Sam dan he'd ever done for de marster.

"I hear'd tell 'bout some Nigger sojers a-plunderin' some houses: Out at Pine Ridge dey kilt a white man named Rogillio. But de head Yankee sojers in Natchez tried 'em for somethin' or nother an' hung 'em on a tree out near de Charity Horspital. Dey strung up de ones dat went to Mr. Sargent's door one night an' shot him down, too. All dat hangin' seemed to squelch a heap o' lousy goin's-on.

"Lawd! Lawd! I knows 'bout de Kloo Kluxes. I knows a-plenty. Dey was sho' 'nough devils a-walkin' de earth a-seekin' what dey could devour. Dey larruped de hide of'n de uppity Niggers an' driv[FN: drove] de white trash back where dey b'longed.

"Us Niggers didn' have no secret meetin's. All us had was church meetin's in arbors out in de woods. De preachers 'ud exhort us dat us was de chillun o' Israel in de wilderness an' de Lawd done sont us to take dis lan' o' milk an' honey. But how us gwine a-take lan' what's already been took?

"I sho' aint never hear'd' bout no plantations bein' 'vided up, neither. I hear'd a lot o' yaller Niggers spoutin' off how dey was gwine a-take over de white folks' lan' for back wages. Dem bucks jus' took all dey wages out in talk. 'Cause I aint never seen no lan' 'vided up yet.

"In dem days nobody but Niggers an' shawlstrop[FN: carpet baggers] folks voted. Quality folks didn' have nothin' to do wid such truck. If dey had a-wanted to de Yankees wouldn' a-let 'em. My old marster didn' vote an' if anybody knowed what was what he did. Sense didn' count in dem days. It was pow'ful ticklish times an' I let votin' alone.

"De shawl-strop folks what come in to take over de country tol' us dat us had a right to go to all de balls, church meetin's, an' 'tainments de white folks give. But one night a bunch o' uppity Niggers went to a 'tainment in Memorial Hall. Dey dressed deysef's fit to kill an' walked down de aisle an' took seats in de very front. But jus' 'bout time dey got good set down, de curtain drapped[FN: dropped] an' de white folks riz[FN: arose] up widout a-sayin' airy word. Dey marched out de buildin' wid dey chins up an' lef' dem Niggers a-settin' in a empty hall.

"Dat's de way it happen ever' time a Nigger tried to git too uppity. Dat night after de breakin' up o' dat' tainment, de Kloo Kluxes rid[FN: rode] th'ough de lan'. I hear'd dey grabbed ever' Nigger what walked down dat aisle, but I aint hear'd yet what dey done wid 'em.

"Dat same thing happened ever' time a Nigger tried to act lak he was white.

"A heap o' Niggers voted for a little while. Dey was a black man what had office. He was named Lynch. He cut a big figger up in Washington. Us had a sheriff named Winston. He was a ginger cake Nigger an' pow'ful mean when he got riled. Sheriff Winston was a slave an', if my mem'ry aint failed me, so was Lynch.

"My granny tol' me 'bout a slave uprisin' what took place when I was a little boy. None o' de marster's Niggers' ud have nothin' to do wid it. A Nigger tried to git 'em to kill dey white folks an' take dey lan'. But what us want to kill old Marster an' take de lan' when dey was de bes' frien's us had? Dey caught de Nigger an' hung 'im to a limb.

"Plenty folks b'lieved in charms, but I didn' take no stock in such truck. But I don't lak for de moon to shine on me when I's a-sleepin'.

"De young Niggers is headed straight for hell. All dey think' bout is drinkin' hard likker, goin' to dance halls, an' a-ridin' in a old rattle trap car. It beats all how dey brags an' wastes things. Dey aint one whit happier dan folks was in my day. I was as proud to git a apple as dey is to git a pint o' likker. Course, schools he'p some, but looks lak all mos' o' de young'n's is studyin' 'bout is how to git out o' hones' labor.

"I'se seen a heap o' fools what thinks 'cause they is wise in books, they is wise in all things.

"Mos' all my white folks is gone, now. Marse Randolph Shields is a doctor 'way off in China. I wish I could git word to' im, 'cause I know he'd look after me if he knowed I was on charity. I prays de Lawd to see 'em all when I die."

United States. Work Projects Administration

Gabe Emanuel, Ex-slave, Claiborne County
FEC
Esther de Sola
Rewrite, Pauline Loveless
Edited, Clara E. Stokes

GABE EMANUEL
Port Gibson, Mississippi

# GABE EMANUEL

Gabe Emanuel is the blackest of Negroes. He is stooped and wobbly from his eighty-five years and weighs about one hundred and thirty-five pounds. His speech is somewhat hindered by an unbelievable amount of tobacco rolled to one side of his mouth. He lives in the Negro quarters of Port Gibson. Like most ex-slaves he has the courtesy and the gentleness of a southern gentleman.

"Lawsy! Dem slav'ry days done been s'long ago I jus' 'member a few things dat happen den. But I's sho' mighty pleased to relate dat what I recollec'.

"I was de house boy on old Judge Stamps' plantation. He lived 'bout nine miles east o' Port Gibson an' he was a mighty well-to-do gent'man in dem days. He owned 'bout 500 or 600 Niggers. He made plenty o' money out o' his fiel's. Dem Niggers worked for dey keep. I 'clare, dey sho' did.

"Us 'ud dike out in spick an' span clean clothes come Sund'ys. Ever'body wore homespun clo'es den. De mistis an' de res' o' de ladies in de Big House made mos' of 'em. De cullud wimmins wore some kin' o' dress wid white aprons an' de mens wore overalls an' homespun pants an' shirts. Course, all de time us gits han'-me-downs from de folks in de Big House. Us what was a-servin' in de Big House wore de marster's old dress suits. Now, dat was somep'n'! Mos' o' de time dey didn' fit—maybe de pants hung a little loose an' de tails o' de coat hung a little long. Me bein' de house boy, I used to look mighty sprucy when I put on my frock tail.

"De mistis used to teach us de Bible on Sund'ys an' us always had Sund'y school. Us what lived in de Big House an' even some o' de fiel' han's was taught to read an' write by de white folks.

"De fiel' han's sho' had a time wid dat man, Duncan. He was de overseer man out at de plantation. Why, he'd have dem poor Niggers so dey didn' know if dey was gwine in circles or what.

"One day I was out in de quarters when he brung back old man Joe from runnin' away. Old Joe was always a-runnin' away an' dat man Duncan put his houn' dogs on 'im an' brung 'im back. Dis time I's speakin' 'bout Marster Duncan put his han' on old Joe's shoulder an' look him in de eye sorrowful-lak. 'Joe', he say, 'I's sho' pow'ful tired o' huntin' you. I' spect I's gwina have to git de marster to sell you some'r's else. Another marster gwina whup you in de groun' if he ketch you runnin' 'way lak dis. I's sho sad for you if you gits sol' away. Us gwina miss you 'roun' dis plantation.' After dat old Joe stayed close in an' dey warnt no more trouble out o' him.

"Dat big white man called Duncan, he seen dat de

Niggers b'have deyse'ves right. Dey called him de 'Boss Man.' He always carried a big whup an' when dem Niggers got sassy, dey got de whup 'crost dey hides.

"Lawsy! I's recallin' de time when de big old houn' dog what fin' de run-away Niggers done die wid fits. Dat man Duncan, he say us gwina hol' fun'al rites over dat dog. He say us Niggers might better be's pow'ful sad when us come to dat fun'al. An' dem Niggers was sad over de death o' dat poor old dog what had chased 'em all over de country. Dey all stan' 'roun' a-weepin' an' a-mournin'. Ever' now an' den dey'd put water on dey eyes an' play lak dey was a-weepin' bitter, bitter tears. 'Poor old dog, she done died down dead an' can't kotch us no more. Poor old dog. Amen! De Lawd have mercy!'

"De Judge was a great han' for 'tainment[FN: entertainment]. He always had a house full o' folks an' he sho' give 'em de bes' o' food an' likker. Dey was a big room he kep' all polished up lak glass. Ever' now an' den he'd th'ow a big party an' 'vite mos' ever'body in Mississippi to come. Dey was fo' Niggers in de quarters what could sing to beat de ban', an' de Judge would git 'em to sing for his party.

"I 'member how 'cited I'd git when one o' dem shindigs 'ud come off. I sho' would strut den. De mistis 'ud dress me up an' I'd carry de likker an' drinks' roun' 'mongst de peoples. 'Would you prefer dis here mint julip, Marster? Or maybe you'd relish dis here special wine o' de Judge's. 'Dem white folks sho' could lap up dem drinks, too. De Judge had de bes' o' ever'thing.

"Dey was always a heap o' fresh meat in de meat house. De pantry fairly bu'sted wid all kin' o' preserves an' sweetnin's. Lawdy! I mean to tell you dem was de good days.

"I 'member I used to hate ever' Wednesday. Dat was de day I had to polish de silver. Lawsy! It took me mos' all day. When I'd think I was 'bout th'ough de mistis was sho' to fin' some o' 'dat silver dat had to be did over.

"Den de war broke out. De marster went 'way wid de sojers an' gradual' de hardness come to de plantation.

"Us never knowed when dem Yankee sojers would come spen' a few weeks at de Big House. Dey'd eat up all de marster's vit'als an' drink up all his good likker.

"I 'member one time de Yankees camped right in de front yard. Dey took all de meat out'n de curin' house. Well sir! I done 'cide by myse'f dat no Yankee gwina eat all us meat. So dat night I slips in dey camp; I stole back dat meat from dem thievin' sojers an' hid it, good. Ho! Ho! Ho! But dey never did fin' dat meat.

"One time us sot fire to a bridge de Yankees had to cross to git to de plantation. Dey had to camp on de other side, 'cause dey was too lazy to put out de fire. Dat's jus' lak I figgered it.

"When de war was over my mammy an' pappy an' us five chillun travelled here to Port Gibson to live. My mammy hired out for washin'. I don't know zackly what my pappy done.

"Lincoln was de man dat sot us free. I don't recollec' much 'bout 'im 'ceptin' what I hear'd in de Big House 'bout Lincoln doin' dis an' Lincoln doin' dat.

"Lawdy! I sho' was happy when I was a slave.

"De Niggers today is de same as dey always was, 'ceptin' dey's gittin' more money to spen'. Dey aint got nobody to make' em' 'have deyse'ves an' keep 'em out o' trouble, now.

"I lives here in Port Gibson an' does mos' ever' kin' o' work. I tries to live right by ever'body, but I 'spect I won't be here much longer.

"I'se been married three times.

"When de time comes to go I hopes to be ready. De Lawd God Almighty takes good care o' his chillun if dey be's good an' holy."

United States. Work Projects Administration

Dora Franks, Ex-Slave, Monroe County
FEC
Mrs. Richard Kolb
Rewrite, Pauline Loveless
Edited, Clara E. Stokes

DORA FRANKS
Aberdeen, Mississippi

# DORA FRANKS

Dora Franks, ex-slave, lives at Aberdeen, Monroe County. She is about five feet tall and weighs 100 pounds. Her hair is inclined to be curly rather than kinky. She is very active and does most of her own work.

"I was born in Choctaw County, but I never knowed zackly how old I was, 'cause none o' my folks could read an' write. I reckon I be's 'bout a hund'ed, 'cause I was a big girl long time fo' Surrender. I was old 'nough to marry two years after dat.

"My mammy come from Virginny. Her name was Harriet Brewer. My daddy was my young Marster. His name was Marster George Brewer an' my mammy always tol' me dat I was his'n. I knew dat dere was some dif'ence 'tween me an' de res' o' her chillun, 'cause dey was all coal black, an' I was even lighter dan I is now. Lawd, it's bean to my sorrow many a time, 'cause de chillun used to chase me 'round an' holler at me, 'Old yallow Nigger.' Dey didn' treat me good, neither.

"I stayed in de house mos' o' de time wid Miss Emmaline. Miss Emmaline's hair was dat white, den. I loved her' cause she was so good to me. She taught me how to weave an' spin. 'Fore I was bigger'n a minute I could do things dat lots o' de old han's couldn' come nigh doin'. She an' Marse Bill had 'bout eight chillun, but mos' of 'em was grown when I come 'long. Dey was all mighty good to me an' wouldn' 'low nobody to hurt me.

"I 'members one time when dey all went off an' lef' me wid a old black woman call Aunt Ca'line what done de cookin' 'round de place some o' de time. When dey lef' de house I went in de kitchen an' asked her for a piece o' white bread lak de white folks eat. She haul off an' slap me down an' call me all kin' o' names dat I didn' know what dey meant. My nose bled an' ruint de nice clean dress I had on. When de Mistis come back Marse George was wid 'er. She asked me what on earth happen to me an' I tol' 'er. Dey call Ca'line in de room an' asked her if what I say was de truf. She tell 'em it was, an' dey sent 'er away. I hear tell dat dey whup her so hard dat she couldn' walk no mo'.

"Us never had no big fun'als or weddin's on de place. Didn' have no marryin' o' any kin'. Folks in dem days jus' sorter hitched up together an' call deyse'ves man an' wife. All de cullud folks was buried on what dey called Platnum Hill. Dey didn' have no markers nor nothin' at de graves. Dey was jus' sunk in places. My brother Frank showed me once where my mammy was buried. Us didn' have no preachin', or singin', or nothin', neither. Us didn' even git to have meetin's on Sund'y less us slip off an' go to some other plantation. Course, I got to go wid de white folks sometime an' set in de back, or on de steps. Dat was whan I was little.

"Lots o' Niggers would slip off from one plantation to de other to see some other Niggers. Dey would always manage to git back' fore daybreak. De wors' thing I ever heard 'bout dat was once when my Uncle Alf run off to 'jump de broom.' Dat was what dey called goin' to see a woman. He didn' come back by daylight, so dey put de Nigger hounds after him. Dey smelled his trail down in de swamp an' foun' where he was hidin'.

"Now, he was one of da biggest Niggers on de place an' a powerful fas' worker. But dey took an' give him 100 lashes wid de cat o' ninety-nine tails. His back was somethin' awful, but dey put him in de fiel' to work while de blood was still a-runnin'. He work right hard 'til dey lef'. Den, when he got up to de end o' de row nex' to de swamp, he lit out ag'in.

"Dey never foun' 'im dat time. Dey say he foun' a cave an' fix him up a room whar he could live. At nights he would come out on de place an' steal enough t'eat an' cook it in his little dugout. When de war was over an' de slaves was freed, he come out. When I saw him, he look lak a hairy ape, 'thout no clothes on an' hair growin' all over his body.

"Dem was pretty good days back in slav'ry times. My Marstar had a whole passal o' Niggers on his place. When any of 'em would git sick dey would go to de woods an' git herbs an roots an' make tea for 'em to drink. Hogweed an' May apples was de bes' things I knowed of. Sometimes old Mistis doctored 'em herse'f. One time a bunch o' us chillun was playin' in de woods an foun' some o' dem May apples. Us et a lot of 'em an' got awful sick. Dey dosed us up on grease an' Samson snake root to clean us out. An' it sho' done a good job. I'se been a-usin' dat snake root ever since.

"De firs' thing dat I 'member hearin' 'bout de war was one day when Marse George come in de house an' tell Miss Emmaline dat dey's gwine have a bloody war. He say he feared all de slaves 'ud be took away. She say if dat was true she feel lak jumpin' in de well. I hate to hear her say dat, but from dat minute I started prayin' for freedom. All de res' o' de women done de same.

"De war started pretty soon after dat an' all de men folks went off an' lef' de plantation for de women an' de Niggers to run. Us seen de sojers pass by mos' ever' day. Once de Yankees come an' stole a lot o' de horses an' somp'in' t'eat. Dey even took de trunk full o' 'Federate money dat was hid in de swamp. How dey foun' dat us never knowed.

"Marse George come home' bout two years after de war started an' married Miss Martha Ann. Dey had always been sweethearts. Dey was promised 'fore he lef'.

"Marse Lincoln an' Marse Jeff Davis is two I 'members 'bout. But, Lawzee! Dat was a long time back. Us liked Marse Jeff Davis de bes' on de place. Us even made up a song 'bout him, but, I 'clare 'fore goodness, I can't even 'member de firs' line o' dat song. You see, when I got 'ligion, I asked de Lawd to take all de other songs out o' my head an' make room for his word.

"Since den it's de hardes' thing in de worl' for me to 'member de songs us used to dance by. I do' member a few lak 'Shoo, Fly', 'Old Dan Tucker', an' 'Run, Nigger, Run, de Pateroller Catch You.' I don' 'member much o' de words. I does 'member a little o' 'Old Dan Tucker.' It went dis way:

'Old Don Tucker was a mighty mean man,
He beat his wife wid a fryin' pan.
She hollered an' she cried, "I's gwineter go,
Dey's plenty o' men, won't beat me so."

'Git out o' de way, Old Dan Tucker,
You come too late to git yo' supper.

'Old Dan Tucker, he got drunk,
Fell in de fire, kicked up a chunk,
Red hot coal got down his shoe
Oh, Great Lawd, how de ashes flew.

'Git out o' de way, Old Dan Tucker,
You come too late to git yo' supper.'

"When de war was over, my brother Frank slipped in de house where I was still a-stayin'. He tol' me us was free an' for me to come out wid de res'. 'Fore sundown dere warnt one Nigger lef' on de place. I hear tell later dat de Mistis an' de gals had to git out an' work in de fiel's to he'p gather in de crop.

"Frank foun' us a place to work an' put us all in de fiel'. I never had worked in de fiel' before. I'd faint away mos' ever'day 'bout eleven o'clock. It was de heat. Some of 'em would have to tote me to de house. I'd soon come to. Den I had to go back to de fiel'. Us was on Marse Davis Cox's place den.

"Two years later I met Pet Franks an' us married. De

Cox's was good folks an' give us a big weddin'. All de white folks an' de Niggers for miles a-round come to see us git married. De Niggers had a big supper an' had a peck t'eat. Us had eight chillun, but aint but three of 'em livin'. Me an' Pet aint been a-livin' together for de las' twenty-three years. Us jus' couldn' git 'long together, so us quit. He lives out at Acker's Fishing Lodge now an' does de cookin' for 'em.

"I never will forgit de Klu Klux Klan. Never will [TR: "I" deleted] forgit de way dat horn soun' at night when dey was a-goin' after some mean Nigger. Us'd all run an' hide. Us was livin' on de Troup place den, near old Hamilton, in one o' de brick houses back o' de house whar dey used to keep de slaves. Marse Alec Troup was one o' de Klu Klux's an' so was Marse Thad Willis dat lived close by. Dey'd make plans together sometime an' I'd hear 'em. One time dey caught me lis'nin', but dey didn' do nothin' to me, 'cause dey knowed I warnt gwine tell. Us was all good Niggers on his place.

"Lawd, Miss, dese here young folks today is gwine straight to de Devil. All dey do all day an' all night is run 'round an' drink corn likker an' ride in automobiles. I'se got a grand-daughter here, an' she's dat wil'. I worries a right smart 'bout her, but it don't do no good, 'cause her mammy let her do jus' lak she please anyhow.

"Den I tells you, de one thing I worries 'bout mos'. Dat is de white folks what lives here 'mongst de Niggers. You know what kinda folks dey is, an' it sho' is bad influence on 'em. You knows Niggers aint s'posed to always know de right from de wrong. Dey aint got Marsters to teach 'em now. For de white folks to come down here an' do lak dey do, I tells you, it aint right. De quality white folks ought-a do somethin' bout it.

"I's had a right hard life, but I puts my faith in de Lawd an' I know ever'thing gwine come out all right. I's lived a long life an' will soon be a hund'ed, I guess. I's glad dat slav'ry is over, 'cause de Bible don't say nothin' 'bout it bein right. I's a good Christian. I gits sort-a res'less mos' o' de time an' has to keep busy to keep from thinkin' too much."

United States. Work Projects Administration

Pet Franks, Ex-Slave, Monroe County
FEC
Mrs. Richard Kolb
Rewrite, Pauline Loveless
Edited, Clara E. Stokes

PET FRANKS
Aberdeen, Mississippi

# PET FRANKS

Uncle Pet, 92 year old ex-slave, is the favorite of Ackers' Fishing Lodge which is situated 14 miles north of Aberdeen, Monroe County. He is low and stockily built. His ancestry is pure African. Scarcely topping five feet one inch, he weighs about 150 pounds. Though he walks with the slightest limp, he is still very active and thinks nothing of cooking for the large groups who frequent the lodge. He has his own little garden and chickens which he tends with great care.

"I knows all 'bout slav'ry an' de war. I was right dere on de spot when it all happened. I wish to goodness I was back dere now, not in de war, but in de slav'ry times. Niggers where I lived didn' have nothin' to worry 'bout in dem days. Dey aint got no sense now-a-days. All dey b'lieves in now is drinkin' an' carousin'. Dey aint got no use for nothin' but a little corn likker an' a fight. I dont b'lieve in no such gwine-on, no sir-ree. Dat's de reason I stays out here by myse'f all de time. I don't want to have nothin' to do wid 'em. I goes to town 'bout once a mont' to git s'pplies, but I don' never fool 'roun' wid dem Niggers den. I gits 'long wid my white folks, too. All da mens an' wimmens what comes out to de club is pow'ful good to me.

"I was born up near Bartley's Ferry right on de river. De way I cal'clates my age makes me 'bout 92 years old. My firs' Marster was name Mr. Harry Allen. He died when I was a boy an' I don't 'member much 'bout him. De Mistis, dat was his wife, married ag'in an' dat husband's name was Marse Jimmy Tatum. Dey was sho' good white folks. My mammy an' pappy was name Martha an' Martin Franks. Marse Harry brung 'em down from Virginny, I thinks. Or else he bought 'em from Marse Tom Franks in West Point. Anyways dey come from Virginny an' I don't know which one of 'em brought 'em down here. Dey did b'long to Marse Tom. I knows dat.

"Bartley's used to be some place. My folks had a big hotel down on de river bank. Dey was a heap of stores right on de bank, too. De river done wash' em all 'way now. Dey aint nothin' lef'. But Lawdy! When I was a kid de boats used to come a-sailin' up de river 'bout once a week an' I used to know de names o' all de big ones. Dey would stop an' pick up a load o' cotton to carry to Mobile. When dey come back dey would be loaded wid all kin' o' gran' things.

"Us chillun had a big time playin' roun' de dock. Us played 'Hide de Switch' an' 'Goose and Gander' in de day time. Den at nighttime when de moon was shinin' big an' yaller, us'd play 'Ole Molly Bright.' Dat was what us call de moon. Us'd make up stories 'bout her. Dat was de bes' time o' all. Sometimes de old folks would join in an' tell tales too. Been so long I forgits de tales, but I know dey was good'ns.

"When I got big 'nough to work I he'ped 'roun' de lot mostly. Fac' is I'se worked right 'roun' white folks mos' all my days. I did work in de fiel' some, but us had a good overseer. His name was Marse Frank Beeks an' he was good as any white man dat ever lived. I don't never 'member him whippin' one o' de slaves, leastways not real whippin's. I do 'member hearin' 'bout slaves on other places gittin' whipped sometimes. I guess Niggers lak dat wished dey was free, but I didn' want to leave my white folks, ever.

"Us had preachin' an' singin'. Dey was some mighty good meetin's on de place. Old Daddy Young was 'bout de bes' preacher us ever had. Dey was plenty o' Niggers dere, 'cause it was a powerful big place. Old Daddy could sho' make 'em shout an' roll. Us have to hol' some of 'em dey'd git so happy. I knowed I had 'ligion when I got baptized. Dey took me out in de river an' it took two of 'em to put me under. When I come up I tol' 'em, 'turn me loose, I b'lieve I can walk right on top o' de water.' Dey don' have no 'ligion lak dat now-a-days.

"All de Niggers on de Tatum place had dey own patches where dey could plant what ever day wanted to. Dey'd work 'em on Satu'd'ys. When dey sol' anything from dey patch Mistis 'ud let 'em keep de money. When de boats went down to Mobile us could sen' down for anything us want to buy. One time I had $10.00 saved up an' I bought lots o' pretties wid it. Us always had plenty t'eat, too. All de greens, eggs, wheat, corn, meat, an' chitlins dat anybody'd want. When hog killin' time come us always have some meat lef' over from de year befo'. Us made soap out of dat.

"When da war broke out I went right wid de Marster

up to Corinth. I stayed up dere in de camp for de longes' time a-waitin' on de sojers an' nussing de sick ones. I never seen much o' de real fightin'. But I heard de cannons roar an' I waited on de sojers what got wounded.

"After dey moved camp de Marster sont me back home to he'p look after de Mistis an' chillun. De 'Federates had some cattle hid 'way in us pasture an' I looked after 'em. One night when I was comin' home I met 'bout a hund'ed Yankees comin' over a hill. Dey saw de cattle an' took 'bout ha'f of 'em. I skidooed. Dey aint kotched me yet.

"After de war de Yankees called deyse'ves 'Publicans. Dey come down here an' wanted all de Niggers to vote de 'Publican ticket. Den, lemme tell you, I went to work for my white folks. Dey was a-holdin' big meetin's an' speakin's, but I was workin', too. On 'lection day I brung in 1500 Niggers to vote de Democrat ticket. De folks what saw us comin' over de hill say us look like a big black cloud. I reckon us sounded lak one wid all dat hollerin' an' shoutin'.

"All my folks was dead soon, an' I went 'bout lak I was in a trance for awhile. I went firs' one place an' den 'nother.

"When I was on de Cox place I met Dora an' us married. Dat was a big weddin' an' a big feas'. Den us moved over to de Troup place an' stayed dere for a long spell. While us was dere I 'member de Klu Kluxers an' all de carryin' on. Dey would dress up in white sheets an' come 'roun' an' scare all de Niggers. Dey'd whip de bad ones. Some of 'em would git cow horns an' put on dey heads.

One time dey chased a Nigger plumb under de house jus' a-playin' wid 'im. Dey was a-bellowin' jus' lak bulls.

"I can't read an' write. I aint got much use for a Nigger wid a little education. I went to school twict. De firs' teacher I had, dey come an' carried to de pen for signin' his old Marster's name. De nex' teacher, dey put in jail for stealin'. So I jus' 'cided twas jus' better for me not to know how to read'n write, less'n I might git in some kinda trouble, too.

"Dora an' me is got three out o' eight chillun livin'. Dora an' me don' live together no more. She likes to stay in town an' I aint got no patience wid city slickers an' dey ways. She stays wid us gal, Nanny. I stays out here. I goes in to see her 'bout once a mont'.

"I don't git lonesome. Lawdee, no'm! I's got my two dogs. Den de white folks is always a-comin' out here. Dey is good to me. Dey is one right pert Nigger woman what lives down de road a-piece. Her name is Katie, an' I goes down dere when I gits tired o' eatin' my own cookin'. She sets a plumb good table, too."

United States. Work Projects Administration

**NETTIE HENRY**
Meridian, Mississippi

# NETTIE HENRY

Nettie Henry, ex-slave, 19th Street, Meridian, Lauderdale County, is 82 years old. She is five feet tall and weighs one hundred pounds.

"De Chil's place was at Livingston, Alabama, on Alamucha Creek. Dat's where I was born, but I jus' did git borned good when Miss Lizzie—she was Marse Chil's girl—married Marse John C. Higgins an' moved to Mer-ree-dian. Me an' my mammy an' my two sisters, Liza an' Tempe, was give to Miss Lizzie.

"I aint no country Nigger; I was raised in town. My mammy cooked an' washed an' ironed an' done ever'thing for Miss Lizzie. She live right where Miss Annie—she was Miss Lizzie's daughter—live now. But den de house face Eighth Street 'stead o' Seventh Street, lak it do now. Day warnt any other houses in dat block. 'Fore de Surrender, dey turnt de house to face Seventh Street 'cause de town was growin' an' a heap o' folks was buildin' houses. I tell you somp'in' 'bout Seventh Street in a minute. Couldn' nobody dat lived in Mer-ree-dian right after de Surrender ever forgit Seventh Street an' where it head to.

"My pappy didn' go wid us to Mer-ree-dian. He b'longed to one set o' white people, you see, an' my mammy b'longed to another. He'd come to see us till de War started, den his folks jus' kinda went to Texas. I don' know why zackly 'cep' maybe it warnt so healthy for 'em 'roun' Livingston. Dey didn' go to de War or nothin'. I 'spec' nice white folks talked 'bout 'em an' wouldn' have nothin' to do wid 'em. So dey took an' went to Texas an' took my pappy wid 'em. But after de War he come back to us, walked mos' all de way frum Texas. He rented some lan' frum Mr. Ragsdale. My pappy built us a shack on dat lan'. It's tore down now, but it was built good. Us all he'ped. I pulled a cross-cut saw an' toted de boards up on de roof on a ladder. De chimley was built out o' mud an' rocks. Den us moved in an' started growin' us somp'in t'eat. Us didn' have no horse an' plow; Yankees done carried off all de horses an' mules an' burnt up ever'dthing lak plows. Us dug up de groun' wide a grubbin' hoe an' raised pun-kins an' plenty o' chickens an' ever'thing.

"Us lived nice. My people was smart. My white people was good white people. Dey warnt brutish; never whupped us or nothin' lak dat. I don' know nothin' 'bout no meanness.

"Mr. Higgins he died pretty soon an' Miss Lizzie went to teachin' school. Her chillun—Miss Annie an' dem—would try to teach us. Den us carried Blue Back Spellers to Sund'y school an' a old Baptist cullud preacher would teach us out o' it. He say, 'de same words is in dis book what's in de Bible. You chillun learn 'em de way dey is fixed for you to learn 'em in dis here Blue Back Speller, den de firs' thing you know you can read de Bible.' Use went to de white folk's church endurin' o' de War an' right after. Any o' de white folks can tell you 'bout Mr. Preacher Hamlin. He was a preacher an' a school teacher mixed.

He had de firs' boardin' school for young white ladies. It's standin' right dare on Eighth [HW: No 7] Street right now. I 'members de firs' one to gragurate[FN: graduate] frum it. Well, Mr. Hamlin 'nitiated my pappy right dare in de white folks's church, de Firs' Baptis' Church; it burnt up long time ago. My pappy was Isam Allbrook. He was de firs' cullud deacon ordained in Mer-ree-dian.

"I was ten years old at de Surrender, but I took notice. Dem was scarey times an' when you is scared you takes trigger-notice. It was nex' to de las' year o' de War 'fore Sherman got to Mer-ree-dian—not Sherman hisse'f but his sojers. Dey burnt up dat big house on Eighth Street hill an' built camps for de sojers in de flower garden. De cap'ns went an' live at Marse Greer's house. Marse Greer had done sunk all de silver in de duck pond an' hid out de horses an' cows in de big cane-brake what used to be on dis side o' Sowashee Creek. But, Lor!, it didn' do no good. Sherman done caught on by dat time 'bout how to fin' things. Dey got ever'thing an' burned Marse Greer's barn. Day lef' de house an' didn' bother de fam'ly 'cause dey called deyse'fs company. De good Lord knows Marse Greer didn' 'vite 'em! But de Cap'ns bein' dere kep' de rip-rap[FN: riff-raff] sojers frum tearin' up ever'thing.

"When word come dat dey was comin', it soun' lak a moanin' win' in de quarter. Ever'body was a-sayin', 'De Yankees is comin'! De Yankees is comin'!' Us chullun was scared, but it was lak Sund'y, too,—nobody doin' nothin'. Us march' 'roun' de room an' sorter sing-lak, 'De Yankees is comin'! De Yankees is comin'!' Dey wouldn' let us out in de big road. Well, dey come. Dey burn up seventy houses an' all de stores. Dey tore up de railroad tracks an' toted off ever'thing dey couldn' eat. I don' un'erstan' nothin' 'bout how come dey act lak dat. Us aint done nothin' to 'em.

"Well things kep' gittin' worse an' worse. After de Surrender Niggers got mighty biggity. Mos' of 'em was glad jus' to feel free. Dey didn' have no better sense. Dey forgot wouldn' be nobody to take care of 'em. Things warnt healthy an' my mammy an' me kep' close to de white folks. 'Course, Tempe she was grown an' could do what she please. She sho' done somp'in' when she married Cal. Dat was de meanes' Nigger! He nail up a board over de gate pos' what say, 'No visitors allowed'. Sho' 'nough didn' no visitors want to go to his house!

"I don' know how come things got so unnatchel after de Surrender. Niggers got to bein all kin' o' things what de Lawd didn' inten' 'em for, lak bein' policemen an' all lak dat. It was scan'lous! 'Course, it was de Yankees what done it. Dey promise to give ever'body forty acres o' lan' an' a mule. A lot of 'em didn' have no better sense dan to believe 'em. Dey'd go 'head an' do what de Yankees 'ud tell 'em. Well, dey didn' give' em nothin', not even a rooster. Didn' give 'em nothin' but trouble.

"I don' know how come Mr. Theodore Sturges' brother was a Yankee. But after de Surrender he come to Merree-dian an' got to be Mayor. Didn' none o' de white folks lak dat. Mr. Theodore didn' lak it hisse'f, but nothin' he could do 'bout it. Things got so bad de Kloo-Kluxes[FN: Klu Klux] started ridin' at night an' sposin'[FN: disposing] o' bad Niggers. Den one Satu'd'y night Mr. Theodore's big sto' got set fiah to an' de Mayor he tried to blame it on de Kloo-Kluxes. 'Course ever'body knowed de Yankees done it. You see de Yankees was a-tryin' to git de Gov'nor to run de Kloo-Kluxes out. Dat was one awful fiah. Near 'bout de whole town burnt up down town an' ever' nice white man was down dare a-fightin' de fiah.

"Plenty o' Niggers was out, too, doin' devlishment. Three of 'em got 'rested an' dey had de trial Monday. In de meantime, all de Yankee-lovin' Niggers had a big meetin' an' de loudes' mouf dere was dat big buck Nigger Bill. He all time call hisse'f Dennis when he don' call hisse'f Clopton. Here dey goes, all het up frum makin' speeches an' a-drinkin', an' packs de courtroom full. When Mr. Patton got up on de stan' an' say, he sho' done hear Bill Dennis say somp'in', Bill he holler out, 'Dat's a lie!' Only he say a bad word dat I wouldn' say. Den Mr. Patton raise up his walkin' stick an' start toward Bill. 'Bout den Bill jerk out his pistol an' shoot at Mr. Patton. He miss Mr. Patton an' hit Judge Bramlette. Yes'm, kilt him corpse-dead right dere on his high pulpit chair!

"'Bout dat time ever'thing bus' loose. Near 'bout all de white gent'mun in de court room take a shot at Bill. He falls, but he aint dead yet. Dey put him in de sheriff's office an' lef two white men wid him. But things was a-happenin' so fas' by dat time dey couldn' stan' it. Dey th'owed Bill out of dat two-story window an' run down to git in de fight. De white folks was plumb wo' out by dat time wid all de devilishment o' de Yankees an' de fool Niggers. Even a mean Nigger got sense 'nough to know when he done gone too far. Dey all git away as fas' as dey could an' scatter over town, den after dark dey come a-creepin' back to de quarters. Dat was sho' de wronges' thing to do. Dat night, all de sho' 'nough white men came a-marchin' out Seventh Street on dey way to de quarters.

"I had did up Miss Lizzie's parlor curtains dat very day an' de boy was puttin' up de mouldin' frame 'roun' 'em when us hear dat trompin' soun'. It didn' soun' lak no ever'day marchin'. It soun' lak Judgement Day. De boy fell off de ladder an' run an' hid b'hind de flour barrel in de pantry. Miss Lizzie was peepin' out 'twixt dem white lace curtains an' I was right b'hin' 'er. I 'spec' Seventh Street was lined wid wimmin-folks doin' jus' what us doin', 'cause dey husban's, sons, an' sweethearts was out dere in dat march-line.

"Well, dat night ended all de troubles. De line done stop at Mr. Theodore Sturges' house' fore it git out far as us. 'Course, ever'body know Mr. Theodore an' Miss Allie was sho' 'nough folks, but dey was bound to have dat Yankee brother o' his'n.

"De yard was plumb full o' white men ready to burn de house right down on Miss Allie's head lessen dey'd give up dat Yankee Mayor. Mr. Theodore come to de door an' say, 'Gent'mun, he aint here.' Aint nobody believe dat. Dey was a-fixin' to bus' on in anyhow, when Miss Allie come out. She come right down dem steps 'mongst all dem mad folks an' say, calm an' lady-lak, 'Gent'mun, my brother-in-law is here, cert'ny. Where would he go for safety 'cepn to his brother's house? But I give you my word dat he gwine stay right here 'till you put him on de firs' train headin' nawth. Den no mo' blood will be spilled.' An' dat's what dey done.

"Yes'm it was all mighty bad, but plenty good things done happen in Mer-ree-dian, too. I'se seen dis town grow frum nothin'. When us come here 'fore de War, dey was hitchin' dey horses to little oak bushes right in de middle o' town where de bigges' stores is now. I was a grown girl by den an' could make horsemint tea for chills an' mullen leaves for fever good as anybody; an' horehound tea for colds, bitter as gall. I jus' now caught up how to cook an' sew.

"I married when I was nineteen years old. I had nine chillun an' five of 'em's still livin'. Dey looks after me right nice, too. My son in Chicago gimme dis house an' I lives here by myse'f. I keeps it nice an' clean jus' lak I learnt how to do frum de white folks where I used to work. I aint never work for no common folks. I tries to live lak a Christian an' do jus' lak Old Mistis say. Den when I die I can go to Heaven."

United States. Work Projects Administration

**Mississippi Federal Writers**
**Slave Autobiographies**
**Smith Hodges, Ex-Slave, Pike County**
**FEC**
**Mrs. W.F. Holmes**

[FANNY SMITH HODGES
Berglundtown, Mississippi]

# FANNY SMITH HODGES

Fanny Smith Hodges lives in Berglundtown, in the northern part of town, in the only Negro settlement within the corporate limits of McComb.

"My name's Fanny Hodges. I was Fanny Smith befo' I was mar'ied. My mammy was Jane Weathersby, an' she b'long ter old man Weathersby in Amite County. He was de meanes' man what ever lived. My pappy was sol' befo' I was born. I doan know nothin' 'bout him. I had one sister—her name was Clara—and one brudder—his name was Jack. Dey said my pappy's name was George. I doan know.

"Mammy said when I was jes big 'nough to nuss an' wash leetle chulluns, I was sol' to Marse Hiram Cassedy an' dat man give me ter his darter, Miss Mary, to be her maid. De Cassedys sho' was good people. I was big 'nough to draw water, an' put it in a tub an' wash Miss Mary, Miss Annie, an' Miss July. I had to keep 'em clean. I had to comb dey hair an' dey would holler an' say I pulled. I was tol' not to let anything hurt dem chulluns.

"I slep' in de Quarters wid de other niggers. Befo' sunup I had to git to de Big House ter dress dem chulluns. I doan' member whut kind of bed I had, but reckin' it was good. I et in de kitchen. Dey fed fine. I et whut de white folks lef', an' sometimes dey had 'possum an' taters. Dey was good.

"Marse Cassedy was a big Judge. He went to all de cou'ts, an' rode in a fine carri'ge with two big horses hitched ter it, an' a driver. He wore fine clo'es an' ever'body said he was a mighty big man. He had lots an' lots of money. I doan know how many acres in his plantation, but he had more'n 50 slaves.

"When Marse Cassedy was gone, his oberseer would be hard on de slaves, but Marse Cassedy would tell him not to be too hard. He never 'lowed his driver to draw de blood when dey whupped. He fed his slaves. Dey all had gardens and he tuk care of us. He had money in every one of us. De oberseers was white men workin' fer wages.

"I was never whupped afte' I went to Marse Cassedy. Slaves was whupped when dey wouldn't work right. Sometimes dey was lazy. De oberseer blowed a horn every mornin' and de slaves knowed to git up, an' when dat horn blowed agin, dey knowed dey must go to de fiel'. Dey blowed de horn at dinner an' night. Afte' supper, we set 'bout an' sing an go places. Sometimes de men would steal off an' go ter other plantations, an' when kotched dey got a whuppin'. If de pataroller got em, dey sho' kotched it. Dey was whupped an' brung back.

"De white folks had big dances in de Big House and de niggers played de fiddle. Dey was fine times. Dey had good things ter eat, an' I allus got some of whut was lef'.

Christmas time de slaves had dances. I could sho' shuffle my feet. Shucks, folks doan dance like dat any more.

"When slaves was sick, dey went to de woods and got roots an' herbs ter doctor 'em wid. If dey had runnin' off of de bowels, dey got red oak barks an' boiled it an' made 'em drink it. It's de best thing right now to cure runnin' off of de bowels. If young gals had pains in dey stomachs dey made tea out'n gum bark and dat would bring 'em 'round. When babies was born, dey had good midwives to wait on 'em. Dat was good money.

"When Miss July got mar'ied dey had two cooks in de kitchen makin' pound cake fer more'n a week, an' pies, an' chicken pie, an' dey killed a hog. Dey had ever'body in de country savin' butter an' eggs fer a long time. I didn' see de weddin' but de yard was full and we had ever'thing to eat.

"My folks was rich. Marse Cassedy went to de War an' he was a big man dere. He was gone a long time. Dey kep' tellin' us de Yankees was comin' and Miss Fanny had her silver put in a bag and hid. Dey had de money put in a wash pot and buried, an' dey ain't found dat money yet. Oh, dey had more money! Didn' I tell you dey was rich? No mam, dey wasn't po' when war was over. Dey had ever'thing. When de Yankees come, dey carried off all de meat in de smokehouse, an' de blanket an' quilts, an' every thing dey wanted, dey he'ped deyse'ves. None of de slaves went wid' em.

"When Marse Cassedy come home he had de oberseer blow de horn 'bout ten o'clock and tol' 'em all dey was freed. He said he'd work 'em fer wages, an' nearly everyone of 'em stayed fer wages. I stayed wid Miss Mary 'bout ten years. Den I mar'ied. No, Jake an' me rid horse back an' went to Magnolia an' got mar'ied. I doan know who mar'ied us—somebody in de cou't house.

"Me an' Jake went to Summit ter live'. We had to work mighty hard. Sometimes I plowed in de fiel' all day; sometimes I washed an' den I cooked, an' afte' 'while, we moved down to de new town. I come here when dis town fust started. I cooked fer Mrs. Badenhauser, while he was mayor of de town. Dey worked me hard. Me'n Jake's had some hard ups an' downs. I had fo' chullun, none of dem livin' dat I know of. I might have some grandchulluns but if I do, dey live up North.

"I'm old an' can hardly git about. I'se got a cancer. De doctor done cut my lef' brest clear offen me, but dat hurts me somtimes yit.

"I niver jined any church 'til 'bout 20 year ago, right here in Berglundtown. My church is Flowery Mount Baptist Church, an' my Brudder Washin'ton is my pastor, an' he is de best preacher what ever lived. No, Marse Cassedy didn't have no church fer de slaves. Dey went to de white folks' church.

"How do I live? Well I gits a pension of fo' dollars a month, an' I try to wash a leetle fer de colored folks, an' den I beg. I can't stay here long but God won't low me to starve. Bless God, he's comin' fer me some day."

Wayne Holliday, Ex-slave Monroe County
Mississippi Federal Writers
Slave Autobiographies
FEC
Mrs. Richard Kolb

[WAYNE HOLLIDAY
Aberdeen, Mississippi]

# WAYNE HOLLIDAY

"I was born an' raised in Aberdeen an' I'se been a railroad nigger fo' mos' of my days. I'se retired now 'cause dey say I too old to work any longer, but shucks, I ain't half dead yet. I was born in 1853 right here close to whar I live now. My folks b'longed to de Hollidays—you know de grand folks of Miss Maria Evans? An' we stayed right dere in de lot whar de white folks lived.

"My pa an' my ma was named Frank an' Sarah Holliday an' de Cunel brung dem wid him frum North Car'lina. Dey was lot niggers an' never worked in de fiel' or lived in de Quarters. My pa was one of de best carpenters in de country. I was too young to work much but sometime I he'ped him 'roun' de house but mos' of de time, I jes played wid my brudders an' sisters an' de white chullun what lived aroun'. We played marbles, ridin' de stick hoss, an' play house jes lak de chullun do now days, but I think we had mo' fun. Dey was fo'teen of us in our family an' we allus had somebody to play wid. An' den li'l Marse Ben, he wa'nt much older dan us.

"Our marster's name was Cunel John Holiday. He got dat title in a war before de slav'ry war. He was too old to fight in dat one, or I spect he'd got another title, lak Gen'ral or somethin'. He an' Miss Julia—dat was his wife—was mighty good to us an' so was Marse Tom and Marse Ben, an' Miss Maria an' all. When de Cunel fust come to Mississippi he bought a plantation in de prairies an' lived dere for a while. But later he 'cided to build him a house in town so he got my pa to he'p him build it an' it was one of de purtiest houses in Aberdeen. It look jes lak it allus did to me now. Co'se dey is worked on it several times since den, but dey ain't changed it at all.

"My mammy did de cookin' for de white folks dere. Dey all thought a lot of her. I never knowed much what slav'ry was 'bout, to tell de truf. De folks never treated us wrong an' chullun in dem days didn' get to run aroun' lak dey do today an' we didn' get to hear no gossip 'bout de other niggers. Since we didn' live in no quarters we didn' hear nothin. Our folks never said nothin' 'cause dey was very well satisfied lak dey was. We never hear of no whuppin's, or runaways either, 'til afte' de War an' when we got older.

"I 'member de War tho'. Marse Tom, he went fust, wid de Van Dorns. He was made a capt'in or somethin' 'cause he was so brave. He fought long wid de fust an' was one of de fust to get hit. Dey brung his body all de way from Richmond, or Virginny, I fergit which, and lawzy, if de Cunel an' de Miss didn' take on somethin' awful. Dey sho' loved dat boy an' so did all of de niggers. Afte' dey buried him dey took his sword an' hung it on de wall of de parlor. I reckin it still dar.

"Marse Ben went afte' dat. He was jes old 'nough to go

but he went an' fought jes de same. He come back when de war was over an' dey was sho' some rejoicin'.

"Time wa'nt much diffrunt den dan it was 'fo de War. We stayed on wid our folks for a long time. Den my pa started gettin' a li'l work here an' dar an' purty soon he got all his chullun started out purty well. We all went to de colored school what dey had down whar de railroad crossin' is now, an' dat was whar I l'arned to read an' write. I didn' marry for a good while an' den I went to work on de I.C. Railroad. I was fust a coal heaver an' den a coach porter. I was faithful to my job an' made good money an' soon built me a house of my own whar I raised my family. I sent all my chullun to school an' dey is doin' well. My wife worked right 'long wid me. She died 'bout two years ago.

"I'se thankful I ain't got no sad mem'ries 'bout slav'ry times an' dat I an' my folks is done as well as dey have. T'is de work of de Lawd."

Wayne Holliday, who lived in slavery times, and whose father was a slave, is 84 years old, a dried-up looking Negro of light tan color, approximately 5 feet three inches high and weighing about 130 pounds, he is most active and appears much younger than he really is. He is slightly bent; his kinky hair is intermingled white and gray; and his broad mouth boasts only one visible tooth, a particularly large one in the extreme center of his lower gum.

Wayne has the manner of a Negro of the old South and depicts, in his small way, the gallantry of an age gone by.

United States. Work Projects Administration

Prince Johnson, Ex-slave, Coahoma County
FEC
Mrs. Carrie Campbell
Rewrite, Pauline Loveless
Edited, Clara E. Stokes

PRINCE JOHNSON
Clarksdale, Mississippi

# PRINCE JOHNSON

"Yes mam, I sho' can tell you all 'bout it 'cause I was dere when it all happened. My gran'pa, Peter, gran'ma, Millie, my pa, John, an' my ma, Frances, all come from Alabama to Yazoo County to live in de Love fam'ly. Dey names was Dennis when day come, but, after de custom o' dem days, dey took de name of Love from dey new owner. Me an' all o' my brothers an' sisters was born right dere. Dey was eleven head o' us. I was de oldes'. Den come Harry, John, William, Henry, Phillis, Polly, Nellie, Virginny, Millie, an' de baby, Ella.

"Us all lived in de quarters an' de beds was home made. Dey had wooden legs wid canvas stretched 'crost 'em. I can't 'member so much 'bout de quarters 'cause 'bout dat time de young miss married Colonel Johnson an' moved to dis place in Carroll County. She carried wid her over one hund'ed head o' darkies.

"Den us names was changed from Love to Johnson. My new marster was sure a fine gent'man. He lived in a big two-story white house dat had big white posts in front. De flowers all' roun' it jus' set it off.

"Marster took me for de house boy. Den I sho' carried my head high. He'd say to me, 'Prince does you know who you is named for?' An' I'd say to him, 'Yes sir. Prince Albert.' An' den he'd say to me, 'Well, always carry yo'se'f lak he did.' To dis good day I holds myse'f lak Marster said.

"On certain days o' de week one o' de old men on de place took us house servants to de fiel' to learn us to work. Us was brought up to know how to do anything dat come to han'. Marster would let us work at odd times for outsiders an' us could use de money for anything us pleased. My gran'ma sol' 'nough corn to buy her two feather beds.

"Us always had plenty t'eat. De old folks done de cookin' for all de fiel' han's, 'cept on Sund'y when ever' fam'ly cooked for dey ownse'fs. Old Mis' 'ud come over ever' Sund'y mornin' wid sugar an' white flour. Us 'ud mos' ingen'ally have fish, rabbits, 'possums, or coons. Lord, chil'! Dem 'possums was good eatin'. I can tas' 'em now.

"Folks dese days don't know nothin' 'bout good eatin'. My marster had a great big garden for ever'body an' I aint never seen such 'taters as growed in dat garden. Dey was so sweet de sugar 'ud bus' right th'ough de peelin' when you roasted 'em in de ashes.

"Old Aunt Emily cooked for all de chillun on de place. Ha'f a hour by de sun, dey was all called in to supper. Dey had pot likker an' ash cake an' such things as would make 'em grow.

"Chillun den didn' know nothin' 'bout all de fancy ailments what chillun have now. Dey run an' played all day in dey shirt tails in de summer time. When winter come dey had good warm clo'es[FN: clothes] same as us older ones.

"One day Marster's chillun an' de cullud chillun slipped off to de orchard. Dey was jus' a-eatin' green apples fas' as dey could when 'long come de master, hisse'f. He lined 'em all up, black an' white alike, an' cut a keen switch. Twant a one in dat line dat didn' git a few licks. Den he called de old doctor woman an' made 'er give 'em ever' one a dose o' medicine. Dey didn' a one of' em git sick.

"Marster an' Old Mis' had five chillun. Dey is all dead an' gone now, an' I's still here. One o' his sons was a Supreme Judge 'fore he died.

"My folks was sho' quality. Marster bought all de little places 'roun' us so he wouldn' have no po' white trash neighbors. Yes sir! He owned 'bout thirty-five hund'ed acres an' at leas' a hund'ed an' fifty slaves.

"Ever' mornin' 'bout fo' 'clock us could hear dat horn blow for us to git up an' go to de fiel'. Us always quit work 'fore de sun went down an' never worked at night. De overseer was a white man. His name was Josh Neighbors, but de driver was a cullud man, 'Old Man Henry.' He wasn't 'lowed to mistreat noboby. If he got too uppity dey'd call his han', right now. De rule was, if a Nigger wouldn' work he mus' be sol'. 'Nother rule on dat place was dat if a man got dissati'fied, he was to go to de marster an' ask him to put 'im in his pocket.' Dat meant he wanted to be sol' an' de money he brought put in de marster's pocket. I aint never known o' but two askin' to be 'put in de pocket.' Both of 'em was sol'.

"Dey had jails in dem days, but dey was built for white folks. No cullud person was ever put in one of 'em 'til after de war. Us didn' know nothin' 'bout dem things.

"Course, Old Mis' knowed 'bout 'em, 'cause she knowed ever'thing. I recollec' she tol' me one day dat she had learnin' in five diffe'ent languages.

"None o' us didn' have no learnin' atall. Dat is us didn' have no book learnin'. Twant no teachers or anything lak dat, but us sho' was taught to be Christians. Ever'thing on dat place was a blue stockin' Presbyterian. When Sund'y come us dressed all clean an' nice an' went to church. Us went to de white folks' church an' set in de gal'ry.

"Us had a fine preacher. His name was Gober. He could sho' give out de words o' wisdom. Us didn' have big baptisins lak was had on a heap o' places, 'cause Presbyterians don't go down under de water lak de Baptis' do. If one o' de slaves died he was sho' give a gran' Christian fun'al. All o' us mourners was on han'. Services was conducted by de white preacher.

"Old Mis' wouldn' stan' for no such things as voodoo an' ha'nts. When she 'spected[FN: inspected] us once a week, you better not have no charm 'roun' yo' neck, neither. She wouldn' even 'low[FN: allow] us wear a bag o' asfittidy[FN: asafetida]. Mos' folks b'lieved dat would keep off sickness. She called such as dat superstition. She say us was 'lightened Christian Presbyterians, an' as such us mus' conduc' ourse'fs.

"Nobody worked after dinner on Satu'd'y. Us took dat time to scrub up an' clean de houses so as to be ready for 'spection Sund'y mornin'. Some Satu'd'y nights us had dances. De same old fiddler played for us dat played for de white folks. An' he sho' could play. When he got dat old fiddle out you couldn' keep yo' foots still.

"Christ'mus was de time o' all times on dat old plantation. Dey don't have no such as dat now. Ever' chil' brought a stockin' up to de Big House to be filled. Dey all wanted one o' de mistis' stockin's, 'cause now she weighed nigh on to three hund'ed pounds. Candy an' presents was put in piles for ever' one. When dey names was called dey walked up an' got it. Us didn' work on New Year's Day. Us could go to town or anywhere us wanted to.

"De mos' fun was de corn shuckin'. Dey was two captains an' each one picked de ones he wanted on his side. Den de shuckin' started. You can't make mention o' nothin good dat us didn' have t'eat after de shuckin'. I still studies' bout dem days now.

"Dey was big parties at de white folks' house, me, all dressed up wid taller[FN: tallow] on my face to make it shine, a-servin' de gues'es[FN: guests].

"One time, jus' when ever'thing was a-goin' fine, a sad thing happened. My young mistis, de one named for her ma, ups an' runs off wid de son o' de Irish ditch digger an' marries 'im. She wouldn' a-done it if dey'd a-let 'r marry de man she wanted. Dey didn' think he was good 'nough for her. So jus' to spite' em, she married de ditch digger's son.

"Old Mis' wouldn' have nothin' more to do wid 'er, same as if she warnt her own chil'. But I'd go over to see 'er an' carry milk an' things out o' de garden.

"It was pitiful to see my little miss poor. When I couldn' stan' it no longer I walks right up to Old Mis' an' I says, 'Old Mis', does you know Miss Farrell aint got no cow.' She jus' act lak she aint hear'd me, an' put her lips together dat tight. I couldn' do nothin' but walk off an' leave her. Pretty soon she called, 'Prince!' I says, 'Yes mam.' She says, 'Seein' you is so concerned 'bout Miss Farrell not havin' no cow, you better take one to 'er.' I foun' de rope an' carried de bes' cow in de lot to Miss Farrell.

"Shortly after dat I lef' wid Old Marster to go to North Carolina. Jus' 'fore de war come on, my marster called me to' im an' tol' me he was a-goin' to take me to North Carolina to his brother for safe keepin'. Right den I knowed somethin' was wrong. I was a-wishin' from de bottom o' my heart dat de Yankees 'ud stay out o' us business an' not git us all 'sturbed in de min'.

"Things went on at his brother's place 'bout lak dey done at home. I stayed dere all four years o' de war. I couldn' leave 'cause de men folks all went to de war an' I had to stay an' pertec' de women folks.

"De day peace was declared wagon loads o' people rode all th'ough de place a-tellin' us 'bout bein' free. De old Colonel was killed in battle an' his wife had died. De young marster called us in an' said it was all true, dat us was free as he was, an' us could leave whenever us got ready. He said his money warnt no good anymore an' he dida' have no other to pay us wid.

"I can't recollec' if he got new money an' paid us or not, but I do 'member ever' las' one o' us stayed.

"I never lef' dat place' til my young marster, Mr. Jim Johnson, de one dat was de Supreme Judge, come for me. He was a-livin' in South Carolina den. He took us all home wid 'im. Us got dere in time to vote for Gov'nor Wade Hamilton. Us put 'im in office, too. De firs' thing I done was join de Democrat Club an' hoped[FN: helped] 'em run all o' de scalawags away from de place. My young marster had always tol' me to live for my country an' had seen 'nought of dat war to know jus' what was a-goin' on.

"I'se seen many a patrol in my lifetime, but dey dassent come on us place. Now de Kloo Kluxes[FN: Ku Kluxes] was diff'ent. I rid[FN: rode] wid' em many a time. 'Twas de only way in dem days to keep order.

"When I was 'bout twenty-two year old, I married Clara Breaden. I had two chilluns by her, Diana an' Davis. My secon' wife's name was Annie Bet Woods. I had six chillun by her: Mary, Ella, John D., Claud William, an' Prince, Jr. Three boys an' two gals is still livin'. I lives wid my daughter, Claud, what is farmin' a place 'bout five miles from Clarksdale. I has' bout fifteen head o' gran'chillun an' ever' las' one of 'em's farmers.

"Things is all peaceful now, but de worl' was sho' stirred up when Abraham Lincoln was 'lected. I 'member well when dey killed 'im. Us had a song' bout 'im dat went lak dis:

'Jefferson Davis rode de milk white steed,
Lincoln rode de mule.

Jeff Davis was a mighty fine man,
An' Lincoln was a fool.'

"One o' de little gals was a-singin' dat song one day an' she mixed dem names up. She had it dat Marse Davis was de fool. I'se laughed 'bout dat many a time. When Mistis finished wid' er she had sho' broke her from suckin' eggs.

"I knows all 'bout what slave uprisin's is, but never in my life has I seen anything lak dat. Never! Never! Where I was brought up de white man knowed his place an' de Nigger knowed his'n[FN: his]. Both of' em stayed in dey place. We aint never had no lynchin's, neither.

"I know all 'bout Booker T. Washington. He come to de state o' Mississippi once an' hel' a meetin' in Jackson. He made a gran' talk. He made mention 'bout puttin' money in de bank. Lots o' darkies made 'membrance o' dat an' done it. He tol' us de firs' thing us had to learn was to work an' dat all de schoolin' in de worl' wouldn' mean nothin' if us didn' have no mother wit[FN: energy & common sense]. It's a pity us aint got more folks lak him to guide us now dat us aint got no marster an' mistis to learn us.

"I's a Nigger what has been prosperous. I made a-plenty cotton an' I teached my chillun to be good blue stockin' Presbyterians. All 'roun' de country I was knowed an' ever'body b'lieved in me.

"Maybe things is better lak dey is today. Mos' folks says so anyway. But if Old Marster were a-livin' I'd be better off. I know dat to be so.

"I can hear 'im say to me new, 'Prince Albert, who is

you named for? Well den hol' yo' head high so folks can see you is quality.'"

United States. Work Projects Administration

**Mississippi Federal Writers**
**Slave Autobiographies**

[HAMP KENNEDY
Mahned, Mississippi]

# HAMP KENNEDY

Uncle Hamp Kennedy, a farmer, 78 years old, weighs about 135 pounds, and is about 5 feet 9 inches high. His head is bald with a little gray fuzz over his ears and growing low toward the nape of his neck. He does not wear spectacles nor smoke a pipe. His face is clean shaven.

Physically active, he does not use a crutch or cane and his hearing, eyesight, and mind appear alert. The old Negro cannot read or write, but he has a remarkable memory. He seems very happy in his little cabin where he and his wife live alone, and his eyes beam with interest when he remembers and discusses slavery times.

"I was jes a little nigger when de War broke out—'bout fo' years ol', my white folks say. I had a sister an' three brudders. My mammy an' pappy was Mary Kennedy an' Lon Kennedy. My mammy was Mary Denham befo' she mar'ied. I was born an' raised at Mahned, Mississippi. Old Miss Bill Griffin was my missus.

"De Yankees sho' come to our house—yes sir, dey did. De fust time dey kotched our hogs an' cut off de hind part an' take hit wid' em. De front part dey lef' in de fiel'.

Dey carries corn in de saddle bags an' throwed hit out to de chickens. Den when de chickens come up to eat dey kotched 'em by de head an' wring hit off an' take all de chickens wid 'em.

"Our white folks buried all dey silver in de groun' an' hid dey hosses in de deep gullies near de plantation. Even dey clo'es an' meat dey hide, an' de soljers didn' find nothin' 'cepin' de hosses, an' dey lef' dey tired ones an' tuk our fresh ones wid' em. Dey burned de fiel's an' orchards so our white folks couldn' he'p feed our soljers none.

"One time I 'member when Aunt Charity an' Winnie McInnis, two niggers on our plantation, tried to swim some of our hosses cross de riber to save 'em frum de soljers an' dey rode 'cross in a little boat. Well, when de hosses got in de middle of de water, up comes a' gator[FN: alligator], grabs one hoss by de ear, an' we ain't neber seed him no mo'.

"When niggers run 'way frum de plantation dey was whupped, but dey had to go to da sheriff to be whupped. De sheriff, he would tie de nigger to a tree an' whup him till de blood run out.

"'Bout de only recr'ation us niggers had in dem days was candy pullin's. We all met at one house an' tol' ghost stories, sung plantation songs, an' danced de clog while de candy was cookin'. Dem was de good old days. Dey don't do dem things no mo'.

"When a nigger died, we had a wake an' dat was diffrunt too frum whut 'tis today. Dey neber lef' a dead nigger 'lone in de house, but all de neighbors was dere an' hoped[FN: helped]. Dey turned de mirrors to de wall 'cause dey say once a long time ago, a nigger died an' three days afte'wards his people looked in a mirror an' dere dey see da dead nigger plain as day in de mirror.

"At da wake we clapped our han's an' kep' time wid our feet—Walking Egypt, dey calls hit—an' we chant an' hum all night 'till de nigger was funeralized.

"If we heerd a little old shiverin' owl[FN: screech owl] we'd th'ow salt in de fire an' th'ow a broom 'cross de do' fer folks say dat 'twas a sign of bad luck, an' a charm had to be worked fas' to keep sumpin' terrible frum happenin', an' if a big owl hollered, we wasn't 'lowed to say one word.

"Fire was 'bout de hardes' thing fer us to keep. Dere wa'nt no matches in dem days, an' we toted fire frum one plantation to 'nother when hit burned out. We put live coals in pans or buckets an' toted it home.

"Sometimes we put heavy waddin' in a old gun an' shot hit out into a brush heap an' then blowed the sparks' til de fire blazed. Ever'body had flint rocks too, but few niggers could work 'em an' de ones dat could allus had dat job to do.

"My gran'mammy come frum South Ca'lina an' libed fust at New Augusta, Mississippi. She used to pick big Catawba leaves an' roll her dough in 'em an' bake hit in a log heap, pilin' ashes over hit. Some called hit ash cakes an' hit sho' was good. Nothin' lak hit dese days—no sir.

"We had plen'y to eat—smoke sausage, beef, home made lard, an'—yes sir, possum when we wanted hit.

"We didn' git any pay fer our work but we had plen'y to eat an' clo'es to wear, our clo'es was coarse but good. Most of 'em was wove on de looms an' our socks an' stockings was knitted by de wimmin. De white folks though, dey wear linen an' fine silk clo'es fer de big times. We made blankets—coverlets, too.

"We had 'bout 60 slaves on our place, an' if a nigger man on one plantation fall in love wid a slave girl on 'nother place, dey jus' come to her plantation an' jump ober de broom an' den dey is mar'ied. De slabes never had preachers lak dey do at weddin's dese days. If de girl didn't love de boy an' he jumped ober de broom an' she didn't, den dey wa'nt mar'ied.

"Dere was no schools in dem days either, an' I can't read an' write today. Some of de white folks taught de younger niggers an' den dey tuk dey lessons an' studied at dey cabin of nights afte' dey had finished work.

"We had prayer meetin's in each others houses durin' de week. One plantation owner built a little church on his place an' de niggers, dey go in de back do' an' sit in de back, an' white folks dey come in de front of de church an' sit. De Presbyterin chu'ch was de only one 'round dere an' dey sprinkled ever'body—jes poured water ober dey heads frum a glass an' den patted hit hit in (demonstrated).

"'Twas funny—one time Joe an' Green, two niggers on our place, et dey supper an' run 'way at night an' afte' dey was kotched, dey tol' us dat when dey was passin' through de woods dat night a great big old gran'daddy owl flopped his wings an' Joe said 'we'd better turn back.' I allus heard hit was bad luck fer to hear a owl floppin' lack dat, but Green said 'twant nothin', jes a old owl floppin', but he jes naturally flopped diffrunt dat night, an' Green walked on 'bout 15 steps an' somebody shot him dead. Joe said he tu'ned back an' run home.

"All our niggers had to have passes to leave de plantation an' when de pataroller kotched 'em wid out'n a pass, de nigger was whupped. Sometimes de plantation owner did hit an' sometimes de sheriff. Dey used a long leather strop cut at de ends.

"We used snake root, hohound weed, life everlastin' weed, horse mint, an' sassafras as medicine.

"When de War was right on us, grub was scarce an' sometimes little niggers only had clabber milk an' dey et it in the trough wid de pigs, an' sometimes dey only had pie crusts an' bread crusts at night when dey et on de cabin flo'. Dem was hard times afte' de War.

"'Nother time one nigger run 'way frum our plantation an' hid by day an' traveled by night so de nigger dogs wouldn't git him an' he hid in a hollow tree. Dere was three cubs down in dat tree an' hit was so slick inside an' so high 'til he couldn't clim' out, an' afte' while de ole bear came back an' throw in half a hog. Den she go 'way an' come ag'in an' throw in de other half. 'Bout a hour later, she came back an' crawl in back'ards herse'f. De nigger inside de tree kotched her by de tail an' pulled hisself out. Hit scared de bear so 'til she run in one direction an' de nigger in 'nother. But de nigger, he run in de direction of his marster's place an' said he'd neber run off again as long as he libed.

"I can't 'member de old songs but dese niggers today

can't sing lak dat neither 'cause dey ain't libed back dere, an' dey can't feel hit lak us old folks. Dem was de good old days allright, an' dey was hard days too."

**JAMES LUCAS**
Natchez, Mississippi

# JAMES LUCAS

James Lucas, ex-slave of Jefferson Davis, lives at Natchez, Adams County. Uncle Jim is small, wrinkled, and slightly stooped. His woolly hair is white, and his eyes very bright. He wears a small grizzled mustache. He is always clean and neatly dressed.

"Miss, you can count up for yo'se'f. I was born on October 11, 1833. My young Marster give me my age when he heired de prope'ty of his uncle, Marse W.B. Withers. He was a-goin' through de papers an' a-burnin' some of 'em when he foun' de one 'bout me. Den he says, 'Jim, dissen's 'bout you. It gives yo' birthday.'

"I recollec' a heap' bout slav'ry-times, but I's all by myse'f now. All o' my frien's has lef' me. Even Marse Fleming has passed on. He was a little boy when I was a grown man.

"I was born in a cotton fiel' in cotton pickin' time, an' de wimmins fixed my mammy up so she didn' hardly lose no time at all. My mammy sho' was healthy. Her name was Silvey an' her mammy come over to dis country in a big ship. Somebody give her de name o' Betty, but twant her right name. Folks couldn' un'erstan' a word she say. It was some sort o' gibberish dey called gulluh-talk, an' it soun' dat funny. My pappy was Bill Lucas.

"When I was a little chap I used to wear coarse low-ell-cloth shirts on de week-a-days. Dey was long an' had big collars. When de seams ripped de hide would show through. When I got big enough to wait 'roun' at de Big House an' go to town, I wore clean rough clo'es. De pants was white linsey-woolsey an' de shirts was rough white cotton what was wove at de plantation. In de winter de sewin' wimmins made us heavy clothes an' knit wool socks for us. De wimmins wore linsey-woolsey dresses an' long leggin's lak de sojers wear. Dis was a long narrow wool cloth an' it wropt 'roun' an' 'roun' dey legs an' fas'n at de top wid a string.

"I never went to no church, but on Sund'ys a white man would preach an' pray wid us an' when he'd git through us went on 'bout us own business.

"At Chris'mus de Marster give de slaves a heap o' fresh meat an' whiskey for treats. But you better not git drunk. No-sir-ree! Den on Chris'mus Eve dey was a big dance an' de white folks would come an' see de one what dance de bes'. Marster an' Mistis laugh fit to kill at de capers us cut. Den sometimes dey had big weddin's an' de young white ladies dressed de brides up lak dey was white. Sometimes dey sont to N'awleans for a big cake. De preacher married' em wid de same testimony[FN: ceremony] dey use now. Den ever'body'd have a little drink an' some cake. It sho' was larrupin'[FN: very good] [HW:?]. Den ever'body'd git right. Us could dance near 'bout all night. De old-time fiddlers played fas' music an' us all clapped han's an' tromped an' sway'd in time to de music. Us sho' made de rafters ring.

"Us slaves didn' pay no 'tention to who owned us, leastways de young ones didn'. I was raised by a marster what owned a heap o' lan's. Lemme see, dey is called Artonish, Lockdale, an' Lockleaven. Dey is plantations 'long de river in Wilkinson County, where I was raised. Dey is all 'long together.

"I's sho' my firs' marster was Marse Jim Stamps an' his wife was Miss Lucindy. She was nice an' sof'-goin'. Us was glad when she stayed on de plantation.

"Nex' thing I knowed us all b'longed to Marse Withers. He was from de nawth an' he didn' have no wife. (Marsters wid-out wives was de debbil. I knows a-plenty what I oughtn' tell to ladies. Twant de marsters whut was so mean. Twas dem po' white trash overseers an' agents. Dey was mean; dey was meaner dan bulldogs. Yes'm, wives made a big diffe'nce. Dey was kin' an' went 'bout mongst de slaves a-lookin' after 'em. Dey give out food an' clo'es an' shoes. Dey doctored de little babies.) When things went wrong de wimmins was all de time puttin' me up to tellin' de Mistis. Marse D.D. Withers was my young marster. He was a little man, but ever'body stepped when he come 'roun'.

"Don' rightly know how it come 'bout. Lemme see! De bes' I 'member my nex' Marster was Pres'dent Jefferson Davis hisse'f. Only he warnt no pres'dent den. He was jus' a tall quiet gent'man wid a pretty young wife what he married in Natchez. Her name was Miss Varina Howell, an' he sho' let her have her way. I spec I's de only one livin' whose eyes ever seed 'em bofe. I talked wid her when dey come in de big steamboat. 'Fore us got to de big house, I tol' her all 'bout de goins'-on on de plantations. She was a fine lady. When I was a boy 'bout thirteen years old dey took me up de country toward Vicksburg to a place call Briarsfield. It mus'-a been named for her old home in Natchez what was called 'de Briars.' I didn' b'long to Marse Jeff no great while, but I aint never fo'git de look of 'im. He was always calm lak an' savin' on his words. His wife was jus' de other way. She talked more dan a-plenty.

"I b'lieves a bank sol' us nex' to Marse L.Q. Chambers. I 'members him well. I was a house-servant an' de overseer dassent hit me a lick. Marster done lay de law down. Mos' planters lived on dey plantations jus' a part o' de year. Dey would go off to Saratogy an' places up nawth. Sometimes Marse L.Q. would come down to de place wid a big wagon filled wid a thousan' pair o' shoes at one time. He had a nice wife. One day whilst I was a-waitin' on de table I see old Marse lay his knife down jus' lak he tired. Den he lean back in his chair, kinda still lak. Den I say, 'What de matter wid Marse L.Q.?' Den dey all jump an' scream an', bless de Lawd, if he warnt plumb dead.

"Slaves didn' know what to 'spec from freedom, but a lot of 'em hoped dey would be fed an' kep' by de gov'ment. Dey all had diffe'nt ways o' thinkin' 'bout it. Mos'ly though dey was jus' lak me, dey didn' know jus' zackly what it meant. It was jus' somp'n dat de white folks an' slaves all de time talk 'bout. Dat's all. Folks dat ain' never been free don' rightly know de feel of bein' free. Dey don' know de meanin' of it. Slaves like us, what was owned by quality-folks, was sati'fied an' didn' sing none of dem freedom songs. I recollec' one song dat us could sing. It went lak dis:

'Drinkin' o' de wine, drinkin' o' de wine,
Ought-a been in heaven three-thousan' yeahs
A-drinkin' o' dat wine, a-drinkin' o' dat wine.'

Us could shout dat one.

"I was a grown-up man wid a wife an' two chillun when de War broke out. You see, I stayed wid de folks til 'long cum de Yanks. Dey took me off an' put me in de War. Firs', dey shipped me on a gunboat an', nex', dey made me he'p dig a canal at Vicksburg. I was on de gunboat when it shelled de town. It was turrible, seein' folks a-tryin' to blow each other up. Whilst us was bull-doggin' Vicksburg in front, a Yankee army slipped in behin' de Rebels an' penned 'em up. I fit[FN: fought] at Fort Pillow an' Harrisburg an' Pleasant Hill an' 'fore I was ha'f through wid it I was in Ba'timore an' Virginny.

"I was on han' when Gin'l Lee handed his sword to Gin'l Grant. You see, Miss, dey had him all hemmed in an' he jus' natchelly had to give up. I seen him stick his sword up in de groun'.

"Law! It sho' was turrible times. Dese old eyes o' mine seen more people crippled an' dead. I'se even seen 'em saw off legs wid hacksaws. I tell you it aint right, Miss, what I seen. It aint right atall.

"Den I was put to buryin' Yankee sojers. When nobody was lookin' I stript de dead of dey moncy. Sometimes dey had it in a belt a-roun' dey bodies. Soon I got a big roll o' foldin' money. Den I come a-trampin' back home. My folks didn' have no money but dat wuthless kin'. It was all dey knowed 'bout. When I grabbed some if it an' throwed it in de blazin' fiah, dey thought I was crazy, 'til I tol' 'em, 'dat aint money; it's no 'count!' Den I give my daddy a greenback an' tol' him what it was.

"Aftah de War was over de slaves was worse off dan when dey had marsters. Some of 'em was put in stockades at Angola, Loosanna[FN: Louisiana], an' some in de turrible corral at Natchez. Dey warnt used to de stuff de Yankees fed 'em. Dey fed' em wasp-nes' bread, 'stead o' corn-pone an' hoe cake, an' all such lak. Dey caught diseases an' died by de hund'eds, jus' lak flies. Dey had been fooled into thinkin' it would be good times, but it was de wors' times dey ever seen. Twant no place for 'em to go; no bed to sleep on; an' no roof over dey heads. Dem what could git back home set out wid dey min's made up to stay on de lan'. Mos' of dey mistis' took 'em back so dey wuked de lan' ag'in. I means dem what lived to git back to dey folks was more'n glad to wuk! Dey done had a sad lesson. Some of 'em was worse'n slaves after de War.

"Dem Ku Kluxes was de debbil. De Niggers sho' was scared of 'em, but dey was more after dem carpet-baggers dan de Niggers. I lived right in 'mongst 'em, but I wouldn' tell. No Ma'm! I knowed 'em, but I dasn' talk. Sometimes dey would go right in de fiel's an' take folks out an' kill 'em. Aint none of 'em lef' now. Dey is all dead an' gone, but dey sho' was rabid den. I never got in no trouble wid 'em, 'cause I tended my business an' kep' out o' dey way. I'd-a been kilt if I'd-a run 'roun' an' done any big talkin'.

"I never knowed Marse Linc'um, but I heard he was a pow'ful good man. I 'members plain as yesterd'y when he got kilt an' how all de flags hung at ha'f mas'. De Nawth nearly went wil' wid worryin' an' blamed ever'body else. Some of 'em even tried to blame de killin' on Marse Davis. I fit wid de Yankees, but I thought a mighty heap o' Marse Davis. He was quality.

"I guess slav'ry was wrong, but I 'members us had some mighty good times. Some marsters was mean an' hard but I was treated good all time. One thing I does know is dat a heap of slaves was worse off after de War. Dey suffered 'cause dey was too triflin' to work widout a boss. Now dey is got to work or die. In dem days you worked an' rested an' knowed you'd be fed. In de middle of de day us rested an' waited for de horn to blow to go back to de fiel'. Slaves didn' have nothin' turrible to worry 'bout if dey acted right. Dey was mean slaves de same as dey was mean marsters.

"Now-a-days folks don' live right. In slav'ry times when you got sick a white docter was paid to git you well. Now all you gits is some no-count paten' medicine. You is 'fraid to go to de horspital, 'cause de docters might cut on yo' stummick. I think slav'ry was a lot easier dan de War. Dat was de debbil's own business. Folks what hankers for war don' know what dey is askin' for. Dey ain' never seen no bloodshed. In war-times a man was no more dan a varmint.

"When my white folks tol' us us was free, I waited. When de sojers come dey turnt us loose lak animals wid nothin'. Dey had no business to set us free lak dat. Dey gimme 160 acres of lan', but twant no 'count. It was in Mt. Bayou, Arkansas, an' was low an' swampy. Twant yo' lan' to keep lessen you lived on it. You had to clear it, dreen it, an' put a house on it.

"How I gwine-a dreen an' clear a lot o' lan' wid nothin' to do it wid? Reckon somebody livin' on my lan' now.

"One of de rights of bein' free was dat us could move 'roun' and change bosses. But I never cared nothin' 'bout dat.

"I hear somebody say us gwine-a vote. What I wanta vote for? I don' know nothin' 'bout who is runnin'.

"I draws a Federal pension now. If I lives' til nex' year I'll git $125 a mont'. It sho' comes in handy. I paid $800 for my house an', if I'd-a thought, I'd-a got one wid mo' lan'. I don' wan' to plant nothin'. I do want to put a iron fence a-roun' it an' gild it wid silver paint. Den when I's gone, dar it will be.

"Yes'm. I'se raised a big fambly. Dem what aint dead, some of' em looks as old as I does. I got one gran-chil' I loves jus' lak my own chillun. I don' rightly 'member dis minute how many chillun I had, but I aint had but two wives. De firs' one died long 'bout seventeen years ago, an' I done what de Good Book say. It say, 'when you goes to de graveyard to bury yo' firs' wife, look over de crowd an' pick out de nex' one.'

"Dat's jus' what I done. I picked Janie McCoy, 'cause she aint never been married b'fore. She's a good cook, even if she does smoke a pipe, an' don' know much' bout nothin'.

"I sho' don' live by no rules. I jus' takes a little dram when ever I wants it, an' I smokes a pipe 'ceptin when de Mistis give me a seegar[FN: cigar]. I can't chew tobacco on 'count my teeth is gone. I aint been sick in bed but once in seventy years.

"I is five feet, five inches tall. I used to weigh 150 pounds, but dis old carcass o' mine done los' fifty pounds of meat.

"Now-a-days I has a heap of misery in my knee, so I can't ride 'roun' no mo'. Durin' de War I got a muskit ball in my hip an' now dat my meat's all gone, it jolts a-roun' an' hurts me worse. I's still right sprightly though. I can jump dat drainage ditch in front of de house, an' I sho' can walk. Mos' every day I walks to de little sto' on Union Street. Dar I rests long enough to pass de time-o-day wid my neighbors. My eyes is still good, but I wears glasses for show an' for seein' close.

"De longer I lives de plainer I see dat it ain' right to want mo' dan you can use. De Lawd put a-plenty here for ever'body, but shucks! Us don' pay no min' to his teachin'. Sometimes I gits lonesome for de frien's I used to know, 'cause aint nobody lef' but me. I's sho' been lef a fur piece[FN: long way] b'hin'. De white folks say, 'Old Jim is de las' leaf on de tree,' an' I 'spec dey's 'bout right."

United States. Work Projects Administration

Sam McAllum, Ex-slave, Lauderdale County
FEC
Marjorie Woods Austin
Rewrite, Pauline Loveless
Edited, Clara E. Stokes

SAM McALLUM
Meridian, Mississippi

# SAM MCALLUM

To those familiar with the history of "Bloody Kemper" as recorded, the following narrative from the lips of an eye-witness will be heresy. But the subject of this autobiography, carrying his ninety-five years more trimly than many a man of sixty, is declared sound of mind as well as of body by the Hector Currie family, prominent in Mississippi, for whom he has worked in a position of great trust and responsibility for fifty years or more.

While this old Negro may be mistaken at some points (the universal failing of witnesses), his impressions are certainly not more involved than the welter of local records. Mrs. Currie states that if Sam said he saw a thing happen thus, it may be depended upon that he is telling exactly what he really saw.

Sam McAllum, ex-slave, lives in Meridian, Lauderdale County. Sam is five feet three inches tall and weighs 140 pounds.

"De firs' town I ever seen were DeKalb in Kemper County. De Stephenson Plantation where I were born warnt but 'bout thirteen miles north o' DeKalb. I were born de secon' o' September in 1842. My mammy b'longed to de Stephensons an' my pappy b'longed to Marster Lewis Barnes. His plantation wasn't so very far from Stephenson. De Stephensons an' Barneses were kin' white people. My pappy were a old man when I were born—I were de baby chil'. After he died, my mammy marry a McAllum Nigger.

"Dey were 'bout thirty slaves at Stephenson. My mammy worked in de fiel', an' her mammy, Lillie, were de yard-woman. She looked after de little cullud chillun.

"I don't recollec' any playthings us had 'cept a ball my young marster gimme. He were Sam Lewis Stephenson, 'bout my age. De little cullud chillun' ud play 'Blin' Man', 'Hidin'', an' jus' whatever come to han'.

"My young marster learned me out o' his speller, but Mistis whupped me. She say I didn' need to learn nothin' 'cept how to count so's I could feed de mules widout colicin' 'em. You give' em ten years[FN: ears] o' corn to de mule. If you give' em more, it 'ud colic' 'em an' dey'd die. Dey cos' more'n a Nigger would. Dat were de firs' whuppin' I ever got—when me an' my young marster were a-spellin'.

"I stayed wid him special, but I waited on all de white folk's chillun at Stephenson. I carried de foot tub in at night an' washed dey foots, an' I'd pull de trun'le bed out from under de other bed. All de boys slep' in de same room.

"Den I were a yard boy an' waited on de young marster an' mistis. Hadn' been to de fiel' den—hadn' worked yet.

"Mr. Stephenson were a surveyor an' he fell out wid Mr. McAllum an' had a lawsuit. He had to pay it in darkies. Mr. McAllum had de privilege o' takin' me an' my mammy, or another woman an' her two. He took us. So us come to de McAllum plantation to live. It were in Kemper, too, 'bout eight miles from Stephenson. Us come dere endurin' of de war. Dat were when my mammy marry one of de McAllum Niggers. My new pappy went to de war wid Mr. McAllum an' were wid 'im when he were wounded at Mamassas Gab Battle. He brung 'im home to die—an' he done it.

"Den de Yankees come th'ough DeKalb huntin' up cannons an' guns an' mules. Dey sho' did eat a heap. Us hid all de bes' things lak silver, an' driv'[FN: drove] de stock to de swamp. Dey didn' burn nothin', but us hear'd tell o' burnin's in Scooba an' Meridian. I were a-plowin' a mule an' de Yankees made me take him out. De las' I seen o' dat mule, he were headed for Scooba wid three Yankees a-straddle of 'im.

"Times were tight—not a grain o' coffee an' not much else. When us clo'es[FN: clothes] were plumb wore out, de mistis an' de Nigger wimmins made us some out o' de cotton us had raised. My granny stayed de loom-room all de time. De other winmins done de spinnin' an' she done de weavin'. She were a' good'n'.

"De M & O (Mobile & Ohio Railroad) were a-burnin' wood, den. Dey couldn' git coal. Dey used taller[FN: tallow] pots 'stead o' oil. De engineer had to climb out on de engine hisse'f an' 'tend to dam taller pots. Dey do diffe'nt now.

"Dey were such a sca'city of men, dey were a-puttin' 'em in de war at sixty-five. But de war end 'fore dey call dat list.

"Mistis didn' have nobody to he'p her endurin' de war. She had to do de bes' she could.

"When she hear'd de Niggers talkin' 'bout bein' free, she wore 'em out wid a cowhide. She warnt a pow'ful-built woman, neither. She had to do it herse'f, 'cause twant nobody to do it for 'er. Dey warnt nothin' a Nigger could do but stan' up an' take it.

"Some folks treated dey slaves mighty bad—put Nigger dogs on 'em. All my white folks were good to dey slaves, 'cordin' to how good de Niggers b'haved deyse'fs. Course, you couldn' leave no plantation widout a pass, or de pateroller'd git you. I aint countin' dat, 'cause dat were somthin' ever'body knowed 'forehan'.

"Dey were a heap o' talk 'bout de Yankees a-givin' ever' Nigger forty acres an' a mule. I don't know how us come to hear 'bout it. It jus' kinda got aroun'. I picked out my mule. All o' us did.

"Times were mighty tough. Us thought us knowed trouble endurin' de war. Um-m-m! Us didn' know nothin' 'bout trouble.

"Dey were so many slaves at McAllum's, dey had to thin 'em out. Mistis put us out[FN: hired us out]. She sent me to Mr. Scott close to Scooba. I were mos' a grown boy by den an' could plow pretty good. Come de surrender,

Mr. Scott say, 'Sambo, I don't have to pay yo' mistis for you no more. I have to pay you if you stay. Niggers is free. You is free.' I didn' b'lieve it. I worked dat crop out, but I didn' ask for no pay. Dat didn' seem right. I didn' un'erstan' 'bout freedom, so I went home to my old mistis. She say, 'Sambo, you don't b'long to me now.'

"Dey bound us young Niggers out. Dey sent me an' my brother to a man dat were goin' to give us some learnin' 'long wid farmin'. His name were Overstreet. Us worked dat crop out, but us aint never seen no speller, nor nothin'.

"Den us went back to Stephenson's, where us were born, to git us age. Old mistis say, 'Sambo, you aint twenty-one yet.'

"She cried, 'cause I had to go back to Mr. Overstreet. But I didn'. My mammy an' me went back to McAllum's an' stayed until a man give us a patch in turn[FN: return] for us he'pin' him on his farm.

"I know 'bout de Kloo Kluxes[FN: Klu Kluxes]. I seen 'em. 'Bout de firs' time I seen 'em were de las'. Aint nobody know zackly[FN: exactly] 'bout dem Kloo Kluxes. Some say it were a sperrit dat hadn' had no water since de war. One rider would drink fo' or five gallons at one time—kep' us a-totin' buckets fas' as us could carry 'em. It were a sperrit, a evil sperrit.

"But folks dat aint acted right liable to be found mos' anytime tied up some'r's: De Niggers were a-havin' a party one Satu'd'y night on Hampton's plantation. Come some men on horses wid some kin' o' scare-face on 'em. Dey were all wropped[FN: wrapped] up, disguised. De horses were kivered[FN: covered] up, too. Dey call for Miler Hampton. He were one o' de Hampton Niggers. He been up to somethin'. I don't know what he done, but dey say he done somethin' bad. Dey didn' have no trouble gittin' him, 'cause us were all scared us'd git kilt, too. Dey carried 'im off wid 'em an' kilt him dat very night.

"Us went to DeKalb nex' day in a drove an' ask de white folks to he'p us. Us buy all de ammunition us could git to take de sperrit, 'cause us were a-havin' 'nother party de nex' week. Dey didn' come to dat party.

"I don't know why dey don't have no Kloo Kluxes now. De sperrit still have de same power.

"Den I go to work for Mr. Ed McAllum in DeKalb— when I aint workin' for de Gullies. Mr. Ed were my young marster, you know, an' now he were de jailor in DeKalb.

"I knowed de Chisolms, too. Dat's how come I seen all I seen an' know what aint never been tol'. I couldn' tell you dat. Maybe I's de only one still livin' dat were grown an' right dere an' seen it happen. I aint scared now nothin' 'ud happen to me for tellin'—Mr. Currie'd see to dat—I jus' aint never tol'. Dem dat b'longed to my race were scared to tell. Maybe it were all for de bes'. Dat were a long time ago. Dey give out things den de way dey wanted 'em to soun', an' dat's de way dey done come down:

"'It started wid Mr. John Gully gittin' shot. Now Mr. Gully were a leadin' man 'mong de white democratic people in Kemper, but dey aint had much chance for 'bout seven years (I disremember jus' how long) on 'count o' white folks lak de Chisolms runnin' ever'thing. Ever'body were sho' it were some' o' de Chisolm crowd, but some folks knowed it were dat Nigger, Walter Riley, dat shot Mr. Gully. (But aint nobody ever tol' de sho' 'nough reason why Walter shot Mr. John Gully.)

"'De Chisolms warnt Yankees, but dey warnt white democratic people. Dey do say de Chisolms an' folks lak' em used to run 'roun' wid de Yankees. Maybe dat's how come dey was diffe'nt. Even 'fore de Yankees come a-tall, when Mr. Chisolm were on us side, he were loud moufed-[FN: mouthed] 'bout it.

"'Mr. John Gully he'p Mr. Chisolm git to be judge, but he turnt out to be worse dan dem he had to judge. Mr. Gully an' de others made 'im resign. I reckon maybe dat's why he quit bein' a Democratic an' started ructions wid Mr. Gully.

"'Come de surrender, Mr. Chisolm, he got to be a big leader on de other side. An' he seen to it dat a lot o' de white democratic men got he'p from votin' an' a lot o' Niggers step up an' vote lak he tol' 'em (dey were scared not to). So de Chisolms kep' gittin' all de big places.

"'A lot o' widders an' folks lak dat what couldn' he'p deyse'fs los' dey homes an' ever'thing dey had. De papers de gran' jury make out 'bout it were stored in de sheriff's office. De sheriff give out dat his office done been broke open an' all dem papers stole.

"'Den Mr. Chisolm's brother got hisse'f p'inted[FN: appointed] sheriff an' make Mr. Chisolm deputy. Dat's when he started runnin' things, sho' 'nough. Nex' thing you know, Mr. Chisolm is de sho' 'nough sheriff, hisse'f.

"'Den he gather all his kin' o' folks 'roun' 'im an' dey make out a black lis'. De folkses names dat were on it were de ones de Chisolms didn' need. It were talked 'roun' dat de firs' name on dat lis' were Mr. John Gully's name. A heap o' Kloo Kluxes' names were on it, too. Mr. Chisolm send de Kloo Kluxes' names to de Gov'nor an' spec' him to do somethin' 'bout runnin' 'em out. But, course, he couldn' do nothin' 'bout dat, 'cause it were a sperrit. But ever' now an' den somebody what's name were on dat lis' 'ud git shot in de back.

"'Afore de 'lection come in November (it mus' a-been in '75) de Niggers had been a-votin' an' doin' ever'thing de Chisolms say. Dey were still a-harpin' back to dat forty acres an' a mule dey were promised what dey aint never got. It were turnin' out to be jus' de same wid ever'thing else Mr. Chisolm had been a-promisin' to give 'em. Dey aint never got none of it. De white democratic folks won dat 'lection.

"'Soon Mr. Chisolm run for somthin' or 'nother an' got beat bad. Den he were mad sho' 'nough. He went to Jackson to see de Gov'nor 'bout it. Soon a heap o' white democratic men in Kemper got arrested for somethin' or nother.

"'Den Mr. John Gully got shot an' ever'body were sho' de Chisolms done it. Ever'body were dat mad. Chisolm an' dem had to go to court. But dey were slippery as eels an' Walter Riley's name come out. (He were a Nigger.) Dey give out at de trial dat Walter were hired to shoot 'im by de Chisolm folks. Dat were not de reason, but dey was blood 'fore folks' eyes by dat time.

"'It got worse dat Satu'd'y when Mr. Gully were buried. Folks all over Kemper done hear'd 'bout it by now, an' by nine o'clock Sund'y mornin', people were a-comin' in over ever' road dat led to DeKalb. Dey all had loaded guns. It were on a Sund'y when all de killin' happened—I mean, de windin'-up killin'. I were dere 'fore a gun were fired. I were dere when de firs' man were wounded.

"'De cullud people had gathered in DeKalb at de Methodis' Church. Dey hadn' a gun fired yet. Mr. Henry Gully goes to de cullud people's church. He walked in at de front door an' took his hat off his head. Dey were a-packed in de house for preachin'. He walked down de aisle 'til he got in front o' de preacher an' he turn sideways an' speak: "I want to ask you to dismiss yo' congregation. Dey is goin' to be some trouble take place right here in DeKalb an' I don't want any cullud person to git hurt." De preacher rise to his feet, ever' Nigger in de house were up, an' he dismiss 'em. (Mr. Henry Gully were Mr. John Gully's brother an' a leadin' man o' de right.)

"'De town were a-millin' wid folks from ever'where. Chisolm an' dem done got in de jail for safety an' Miss Cornelia Chisolm went back'ards an' for'ards to de jail. Dey thought she were a-carryin' ammunition in her clo'es[FN: clothes] to her father. Mr. McClendon—he were one of' em—were wid her twict. He were on de right-hand side. Some b'lieved he were de one dat killed Mr. John Gully. Dey tol' 'im dey'd burn his house down if he stay in it, but if he'd go on to jail, dey'd give 'im a fair trial.

"'Well, Mr. McClendon were shot down 'side Miss Cornelia. I seen him when he fell on his face. De man dat fired de gun turn him over an' say, "Well, us got' im." Miss Cornelia run on to de jail where de bounce[FN: balance] o' de fam'ly were.

"'Dem outside say, "Boys, it'll never do! Dey aint all in dere yet. Let's sen' to Scooba an' git Charlie Rosenbaum an' John Gilmore to come help dey frien's. Dey b'longs to dat Chisolm crowd an' we want dem, too."

"'So dey come. Somebody say, "Let's commence right here." I never seen a battle b'fore, but I sho' seen one den. It were lak dis: Mr. Cal Hull was de only democratic white frien' Mr. Rosenbaum had. He stood' twixt his white democratic frien's an' Mr. Rosenbaum. He put his arms over Mr. Rosenbaum an' say, "Boys, he's a frien' o' mine. If you kill him, you kill me." Mr. Rosenbaum crawled over to de courthouse wall, an' squatted down, an' stayed dere. Mr. Hull stood over 'im, pertectin' 'im. But Mr. John Gilmore make for de jail an', when dey open de door for 'im, de shootin' start. Right den were when Mr. Gilmore got his. Miss Cornelia were struck in de wris'. It mortified an' after 'while she died from it.'

"I know I aint tol' de sho' 'nough reason Mr. John Gully got killed. Maybe de time done come for de truf to be tol'. Hope won't nobody think hard o' me for tellin':

"Mr. John Gully had a bar-room an' a clerk. A white man by de name o' Bob Dabbs walked[FN: clerked] b'hin' dat counter. Dis Nigger, Walter Riley, I was a-tellin' you 'bout awhile ago, were a-courtin' a yaller[FN: yellow] woman. (Dey warnt so many of 'em in dem days.) Mr. Dabbs say, "Walter, if I ever kotch[FN: catch] you walkin wid (he called dat yaller woman's name) I'll give you de worst beatin' ever was." Walter were kotch wid 'er ag'in. Dat Frid'y night he come a-struttin' into de bar-room. Mr. Dabbs say, "Come he'p move dese boxes here in de nex' room." Walter walked in lak a Nigger will when you ask 'im to do somethin', an' Mr. Dabbs turnt de key. "Git 'crost dat goods box," he say. "I'll give you what I promised you." Mr. Dabbs got 'im a piece o' plank an' burnt Walter up.

"All dis here were a-goin' on 'bout de time Niggers were a-votin' an' doin' things 'roun' white folks. Dey thought dey were pertected by de Chisolm crowd.

"De nex' Frid'y night Walter walked right into dat bar-room ag'in. Mr. Dabbs say, "What you doin' here, Nigger?" Walter say, "You 'member what you done to me tonight one week?" An' he say, "Well, what's to it?" Den Walter say, "Well, I come to settle wid you." Mr. Dabbs say, "Let me see if I can't hurry you up some," an' he retch[FN: reached] his han' back his han' to his hip. But 'fore he could draw[FN: draw his gun] out, Walter done run back to de door. Dey were a chinaberry tree close to de door an' Walter got b'hin' it an' fired a pistol. Mr. Dabbs were hit wid his arm a-layin' 'crost de counter wid his pistol in his han'.

"'Me an' Mr. Ed ('cause he were de jailor), we put him on a mattress in de room back o' de bar. An' he died dat night. De word jus' kinda got' roun' dat some of de Chisolm crowd done killed Mr. Gully's clerk.

"'Walter run off to Memphis. Mr. Gully were pursuin' after 'im to ketch 'im. Walter sho' got tired of him pursuin' after 'im. Dat were de evidence Walter give out 'fore dey put de rope on his neck an' start him on his way to de gallows, but twant nobody dere to put it down jus' lak it were.

"'Mr. Sinclair were sheriff by dis time, an' my young marster an' me went wid 'im to git Walter to take 'im to de gallows. Mr. Sinclair say, "Ed, you goin' to de jail-house now? Here's a ha'f pint o' whiskey. Give it to Walter, make 'im happy, den if he talk too much, nobody will b'lieve it." Mr. Ed say, "Come on, Sambo, go wid me." He retched down an' got a han'ful o' goobers an' put 'em in his pocket. We were eatin' 'em on de way down to de jail-house. He say, "Walter, Mr. Sinclair done sent you a dram." Walter say, "Mr. McAllum, I see you an' Sam eatin' peanuts comin' along. Jus' you give me a han'ful an' I'll eat dem on de way to de gallows. I don't want no whiskey."

"'Den us got on de wagon. (I can see Walter now, standin' dere wid his cap on de back o' his head ready to pull down over his eyes after he git dere.) Dey were a pow'ful crowd 'roun' dat wagon.

"'Den come a rider from Scooba, pull a paper from his pocket, an' han' it to Mr. Sinclair. He read it an' say," Let de people go on to de gallows. De wagon turn 'roun' an' go back to de jail." De Gov'nor had stopped de hangin' 'til de case were 'vestigated. (De people standin' dere a-waitin' for Walter to be hung didn' know what were de matter.)

"'Dey placed Walter back in jail an' his coffin 'long wid' im. De lawyers would visit 'im to git his testimony. Dey'd show 'im his coffin all ready an' ask him did he do dis killin' or not. Dey want 'im to say he were hired to do it. Dey fixed it all up. Twant nobody to tell jus' how it were.'

"I were married by dis time to Laura. She were de nurse maid to Mr. J.H. Currie. She's been dead twenty years, now. When de Curries come to Meridian to live, dey give me charge o' dey plantation. I were de leader an' stayed an' worked de plantation for' em. Dey been livin' in Meridian twelve years. I's married now to dey cook.

"Mr. Hector tol' me if I'd come an' live wid' em here, he'd gimme dis house here in de back yard an' paint it an' fix it all up lak you see it. It's mighty pleasant in de shade. Folks used to always set dey houses in a grove, but now dey cuts down more trees dan dey keeps. Us don't cut no trees. Us porches is always nice an' shady.

"I'se got fo' boys livin'. One son were in de big strike in de automobile plant in Detroit an' couldn' come to see me las' Chris'mus. He'll come to see me nex' year if I's still here.

"Maybe folks goin' a-think hard o' me for tellin' what aint never been tol' b'fore. I been asked to tell what I seen an' I done it.

"Dat's tellin' what I never thought to tell."

United States. Work Projects Administration

Charlie Moses, Ex-slave, Lincoln County
FEC
Esther de Sola
Rewrite, Pauline Loveless
Edited, Clara E. Stokes

**CHARLIE MOSES**
Brookhaven, Mississippi

# CHARLIE MOSES

Charlie Moses, 84 year old ex-slave, lives at Brookhaven. He possesses the eloquence and the abundant vocabulary of all Negro preachers. He is now confined to his bed because of the many ailments of old age. His weight appears to be about 140 pounds, height 6 feet 1 inch high.

"When I gits to thinkin' back on them slavery days I feels like risin' out o' this here bed an' tellin' ever'body 'bout the harsh treatment us colored folks was given when we was owned by poor quality folks.

"My marster was mean an' cruel. I hates him, hates him! The God Almighty has condemned him to eternal fiah. Of that I is certain. Even the cows and horses on his plantation was scared out o' their minds when he come near 'em. Oh Lordy! I can tell you plenty 'bout the things he done to us poor Niggers. We was treated no better than one o' his houn' dogs. Sometimes he didn' treat us as good as he did them. I prays to the Lord not to let me see him when I die. He had the devil in his heart.

"His name was Jim Rankin an' he lived out on a plantation over in Marion County. I was born an' raised on his place. I spec I was 'bout twelve year old at the time o' the war.

"Old man Rankin worked us like animals. He had a right smart plantation an' kep' all his Niggers, 'cept one house boy, out in the fiel' a-workin'. He'd say, 'Niggers is meant to work. That's what I paid my good money for 'em to do.'

"He had two daughters an' two sons. Them an' his poor wife had all the work in the house to do, 'cause he wouldn' waste no Nigger to help 'em out. His family was as scared o' him as we was. They lived all their lives under his whip. No Sir! No Sir! There warnt no meaner man in the world than old man Jim Rankin.

"My pappy was Allen Rankin an' my mammy was Ca'line. There was twelve o' us chillun, nine boys an' three girls. My pa was born in Mississippi an' sol' to Marster Rankin when he was a young man. My mammy was married in South Carolina an' sol' to Marster Rankin over at Columbia. She had to leave her family. But she warnt long in gittin' her another man.

"Oh Lordy! The way us Niggers was treated was awful. Marster would beat, knock, kick, kill. He done ever'thing he could 'cept eat us. We was worked to death. We worked all Sunday, all day, all night. He whipped us 'til some jus' lay down to die. It was a poor life. I knows it aint right to have hate in the heart, but, God Almighty! It's hard to be forgivin' when I think of old man Rankin.

"If one o' his Niggers done something to displease

him, which was mos' ever' day, he'd whip him' til he'd mos' die an' then he'd kick him 'roun in the dust. He'd even take his gun an', before the Nigger had time to open his mouth, he'd jus' stan' there an' shoot him down.

"We'd git up at dawn to go to the fiel's. We'd take our pails o' grub with us an' hang' em up in a row by the fence. We had meal an' pork an' beef an' greens to eat. That was mos'ly what we had. Many a time when noontime come an' we'd go to eat our vittals the marster would come a-walkin' through the fiel with ten or twelve o' his houn' dogs. If he looked in the pails an' was displeased with what he seen in 'em, he took 'em an' dumped 'em out before our very eyes an' let the dogs grab it up. We didn' git nothin' to eat then 'til we come home late in the evenin'. After he left we'd pick up pieces of the grub that the dogs left an' eat 'em. Hongry—hongry—we was so hongry.

"We had our separate cabins an' at sunset all of us would go in an' shut the door an' pray the Lord Marster Jim didn' call us out.

"We never had much clothes 'ceptin' what was give us by the marster or the mistis. Winter time we never had 'nough to wear nor 'nough to eat. We wore homespun all the time. The marster didn' think we needed anything, but jus' a little.

"We didn' go to church, but Sundays we'd gather 'roun' an' listen to the mistis read a little out o' the Bible. The marster said we didn' need no religion an' he finally stopped her from readin' to us.

"When the war come Marster was a captain of a regiment. He went away an' stayed a year. When he come back he was even meaner than before.

"When he come home from the war he stayed for two weeks. The night 'fore he was a-fixin' to leave to go back he come out on his front porch to smoke his pipe. He was a-standin' leanin' up ag'in' a railin' when somebody sneaked up in the darkness an' shot him three times. Oh my Lord! He died the nex' mornin'. He never knowed who done it. I was glad they shot him down.

"Sometimes the cavalry would come an' stay at the house an' the mistis would have to 'tend to 'em an' see that they got plenty to eat an' fresh horses.

"I never seen no fightin'. I stayed on the plantation 'til the war was over. I didn' see none o' the fightin'.

"I don't 'member nothin' 'bout Jefferson Davis. Lincoln was the man that set us free. He was a big general in the war.

"I 'member a song we sung, then. It went kinda like this:

'Free at las',
Free at las',
Thank God Almighty
I's free at las'.
Mmmmm, mmmmm, mmmmm.'

"I only seen the Klu Klux Klan onct. They was a-paradin' the streets here in Brookhaven. They had a Nigger that they was a-goin' to tar an' feather.

"When the mistis tol' us we was free (my pappy was

already dead, then) my mammy packed us chillun up to move. We travelled on a cotton wagon to Covington, Louisiana. We all worked on a farm there 'bout a year. Then all 'cept me moved to Mandeville, Louisiana an' worked on a farm there. I hired out to Mr. Charlie Duson, a baker. Then we moved to a farm above Baton Rouge, Louisiana an' worked for Mr. Abe Manning. We jus' travelled all over from one place to another.

"Then I got a letter from a frien' o' mine in Gainesville, Mississippi. He had a job for me on a boat, haulin' lumber up the coast to Bay St. Louis, Pass Christian, Long Beach, Gulfport, an' all them coast towns. I worked out o' Gainesville on this boat for 'bout two year. I lost track o' my family then an' never seen 'em no more.

"In the year 1870 I got the call from the Lord to go out an' preach. I left Gainesville an' travelled to Summit, Mississippi where another frien' o' mine lived. I preached the words of the Lord an' travelled from one place to another.

"In 1873 I got married an' decided to settle in Brookhaven. I preached an' all my flock believed in me. I bought up this house an' the two on each side of it. Here I raised seven chillun in the way o' the Lord. They is all in different parts of the country now, but I sees one of 'em ever' now an' then. Las' April the Lord seen fit to put me a-bed an' I been ailin' with misery ever since.

"The young folks now-a-days are happy an' don't know' bout war an' slavery times, but I does. They don't know nothin' an' don't make the mark in the worl' that the old folks did. Old people made the first roads in Mississippi. The Niggers today wouldn' know how to act on a plantation. But they are happy. We was miserable.

"Slavery days was bitter an' I can't forgit the sufferin'. Oh, God! I hates 'em, hates 'em. God Almighty never meant for human beings to be like animals. Us Niggers has a soul an' a heart an' a min'. We aint like a dog or a horse. If all marsters had been good like some, the slaves would all a-been happy. But marstars like mine ought never been allowed to own Niggers.

"I didn' spec nothin' out of freedom 'ceptin' peace an' happiness an' the right to go my way as I pleased. I prays to the Lord for us to be free, always.

"That's the way God Almighty wants it."

Henri Necaise, Ex-Slave, Pearl River County
FEC
Mrs. C.E. Wells
Rewrite, Pauline Loveless
Edited, Clara E. Stokes

HENRI NECAISE
Nicholson, Mississippi

# HENRI NECAISE

Henri Necaise, ex-slave, 105 years old, lives a half-mile south of Nicholson on US 11. Uncle Henri lives in a small plank cabin enclosed by a fence. He owns his cabin and a small piece of land. He is about five feet ten inches tall and weighs 120 pounds. His sight and hearing are very good.

"I was born in Harrison County, 19 miles from Pass Christian, 'long de ridge road from de swamp near Wolf River. My Marster was Ursan Ladnier. De Mistis' name was Popone. Us was all French. My father was a white man, Anatole Necaise. I knowed he was my father, 'cause he used to call me to him an' tell me I was his oldes' son.

"I never knowed my mother. I was a slave an' my mother was sol' from me an' her other chilluns. Dey tol' me when dey sol' 'er my sister was a-holdin' me in her arms. She was standin' behin' da Big House peekin' 'roun' de corner an' seen de las' of her mother. I seen her go, too. Dey tell me I used to go to de gate a-huntin' for my mammy. I used to sleep wid my sister after dat.

"Jus' lemme study a little, an' I'll tell you 'bout de Big House. It was 'bout 60 feet long, built o' hewed logs, in two parts. De floors was made o' clay dey didn' have lumber for floors den. Us lived right close to de Big House in a cabin. To tell de truf, de fac' o' de business is, my Marster took care o' me better'n I can take care o' myse'f now.

"When us was slaves Marster tell us what to do. He say, 'Henri, do dis, do dat.' An' us done it. Den us didn' have to think whar de nex' meal comin' from, or de nex' pair o' shoes or pants. De grub an' clo'es give us was better'n I ever gits now.

"Lemme think an' counts. My Marster didn' have a lot o' slaves. Dere was one, two, three, fo', yes'm, jus' fo' o' us slaves. I was de stockholder. I tended de sheep an' cows an' such lak. My Marster didn' raise no big crops, jus' corn an' garden stuff. He had a heap o' cattle. Dey could run out in de big woods den, an' so could de sheeps. He sol' cattle to N'awlins[FN: New Orleans] an' Mobile, where he could git de bes' price. Dat's de way folks does now, aint it? Dey sells wherever dey can git de mos' money.

"Dey didn' give me money, but, you see, I was a slave. Dey sho' give me ever'thing else I need, clo'es an' shoes. I always had a-plenty t'eat, better'n I can git now. I was better off when I was a slave dan I is now, 'cause I had ever'thing furnished me den. Now I got to do it all myse'f.

"My Marster was a Catholic. One thing I can thank dem godly white folks for, dey raise' me right. Dey taught me out o' God's word, 'Our Father which art in Heaven.' Ever'body ought-a know dat prayer."

(Note. In this Wolf River territory in Harrison County, where Uncle Henri was born and raised, all the settlers were French Catholics, and it was the scene of early Catholic missions.)

"I was rais' a Catholic, but when I come here twant no church an' I joined de Baptis' an' was baptised. Now de white folks lemme go to dey church. Dey aint no cullud church near 'nough so's I can go. I spec' its all right. I figgers dat God is ever'where.

"My Mistis knowed how to read an' write. I don' know 'bout de Marster. He could keep sto' anyway. Us all spoke French in dem days. I near 'bout forgit all de songs us used to sing. Dey was all in French anyway, an' when you don' speak no French for 'bout 60 years, you jus' forgit it.

"I'se knowed slaves to run away, an' I'se seen 'em whupped. I seen good marsters an' mean ones. Dey was good slaves an' mean ones. But to tell de truf, if dey tol' a slave to do anything, den he jus' better do it.

"I was big' nough in de Civil War to drive five yoke o' steers to Mobile an' git grub to feed de wimmins an' chilluns. Some o' de mens was a-fightin' an' some was a-runnin' an' hidin'. I was a slave an' I had to do what dey tol' me. I carried grub into de swamp to men, but I never knowed what dey was a-hidin' from."

(This may be explained by the fact that Uncle Henri was owned by and lived in a settlement of French People, many of whom probably had no convictions or feeling of loyalty, one way or the other, during the War Between the States.)

"My old Marster had fo' sons, an' de younges' one went to de war an' was killed.

"De Yankees come to Pass Christian, I was dere, an' seen 'em. Dey come up de river an' tore up things as dey went along.

"I was 31 years old when I was set free. My Marster didn' tell us' bout bein' free. De way I foun' it out, he started to whup me once an' de young Marster up an' says, 'You aint got no right to whup him now, he's free.' Den Marster turnt me loose.

"It was dem Carpetbaggers dat 'stroyed de country. Dey went an' turned us loose, jus' lak a passel o' cattle, an' didn' show us nothin' or giv' us nothin'. Dey was acres an' acres o' lan' not in use, an' lots o' timber in dis country. Dey should-a give each one o' us a little farm an' let us git out timber an' build houses. Dey ought to put a white Marster over us, to show us an' make us work, only let us be free 'stead o' slaves. I think dat would-a been better 'n turnin' us loose lak dey done.

"I lef' my Marster an' went over to de Jordon River, an' dere I stayed an' worked. I saved my money an' dat giv' me a start. I never touched it' til de year was winded up. To tell da truf, de fac's o' de matter is, it was my Marstars kinfolks I was workin' for.

"I bought me a schooner wid dat money an' carried charcoal to N'awlins. I done dis for 'bout two years an' den I los' my schooner in a storm off o' Bay St. Louis.

"After I los' my schooner, I come here an' got married. Dis was in 1875 an' I was 43 years old. Dat was my firs' time to marry. I'se got dat same wife today. She was born a slave, too. I didn' have no chillun, but my wife did. She had one gal-chil'. She lives at Westonia an' is de mammy o' ten chillun. She done better'n us done. I'se got a lot o' gran'-chillun. What does you call de nex' den? Lemme see, great gran'-chillun, dat's it.

"I never did b'lieve in no ghos' an' hoodoos an' charms.

"I never did look for to git nothin' after I was free. I had dat in my head to git me 80 acres o' lan' an' homestead it. As for de gov'ment making me a present o' anything, I never thought 'bout it. But jus' now I needs it.

"I did git me dis little farm, 40 acres, but I bought it an' paid for it myse'f. I got de money by workin' for it. When I come to dis country I dug wells an' built chimneys on' houses. (Once I dug a well 27 feet an' come to a coal bed. I went through de coal an' foun' water. Dat was on de Jordon River.) Dat clay chimney an' dis here house has been built 52 years. I's still livin' in' em. Dey's mine. One acre, I giv' to de Lawd for a graveyard an' a churchhouse. I wants to be buried dere myse'f.

"A white lady paid my taxes dis year. I raises a garden an' gits de Old Age 'Sistance. It aint 'nough to buy grub an' clo'es for me an' de old woman an' pay taxes, so us jus' has to git 'long de bes' us can wid de white folks he'p.

"It aint none o' my business' bout whether de Niggers is better off free dan slaves. I dont know 'cept 'bout me, I was better off den. I did earn money after I was free, but after all, you know money is de root o' all evil. Dat what de Good Book say. When I was a slave I only had to obey my Marster an' he furnish me ever'thing. Once in a while he would whup me, but what was dat? You can't raise nary chile, white or black, widout chastisin'. De law didn' low dem to dominize over us, an' dey didn' try.

"I's gittin' mighty old now, but I used to be pretty spry. I used to go 60 miles out on de Gulf o' Mexico, as 'terpreter on dem big ships dat come from France. Dat was 'fore I done forgot my French talk what I was raised to speak.

"De white folks is mighty good to me. De riches' man in Picayune, he recognizes me an' gives me two bits or fo' bits. I sho' has plenty o' good frien's. If I gits out o' grub, I catches me a ride to town, an' I comes back wid de grub.

"De good Lawd, he don't forgit me."

**Mississippi Federal Writers**
**Slave Autobiographies**

[REV. JAMES SINGLETON
Simpson, Mississippi]

# JAMES SINGLETON

"My name's James Singleton. I'se a Baptist preacher. I was born in 1856, but I doan know zactly what date. My mammy was Harr'et Thompson. Her marster was Marse Daniel Thompson over in Simpson County on Strong River at a place called Westville. My pappy, he come from South Ca'lina—Charleston—an' was give to do old folks' darter. His name was John Black an' he was owned by Mr. Frank Smith over in Simpson. He was brought down frum South Ca'lina in a wagon 'long wid lots mo'.

"Me, I was sol' to Marse Harrison Hogg over in Simpson when I was 'bout six years old, and Marse Hogg, he turn right 'roun', and sol' me an' sister Harr'et an' brother John nex' day for fo' thousan'. Two thousan' fo' John, 'cause he's older an' bigger, an' a thousan' fo' Harr'et an' me. Miss Annie an' Marse Elbert Bell bought us.

"Marse Elbert had three mo' sides us—makin' six. Us slep' on pallets on de flo', an' all lived in one long room made out of logs, an' had a dirt flo' an' dirt chimbly. There was a big old iron pot hangin' over de hearth, an' us had 'possum, greens, taters, and de lak cooked in it. Had coon sometimes, too.

"Marse Elbert, he lived in jes a plain wood house made Califo'nia style, wid a front room an' a shed room where de boys slep'. Dey had two boys, Jettie an' William.

"I reckin dere was 'bout a hun'erd an' sixty acres planted in taters an' corn, an' dey made whiskey too. Yessum, dey had a 'stillery[FN: distillery] hid down in de woods where dey made it.

"My mammy an' pappy was fiel' han's, an' I was mighty little to do so much. I jes minded de cow pen, made fires in de Big House, an' swep' de house. When I made de fires, iffen dere wa'nt any live coale lef', we had to use a flint rock to git it sta'ted.

"Dere was a bell ringin' every mornin' 'bout fo' 'clock, fer to call de slaves tar git up an' go to de fiel's. Day wuked 'til sundown. Dey was fed in de white folks' kitchen, and Cook cooked fer us jes lak she done fer de whites. De kitchen was built off a piece frum de hous', y'know.

"Marse never did whup any of us li'l chullun. Miss Annie, she tried once to whup me 'cause I chunked rocks at her li'l chickens, but mighty little whuppin' she done. Dere wa'nt no overseer.

"Chris'mas time, we had two or three days to play, an' had extry food.

"I seen 'pattyrollers' ridin' 'bout to keep de darkies from runnin' 'roun' widout passes. I never seen 'em whup none but dey tol' us we'd git twen'y-nine licks iffen we got caught by 'em. I seen darkies git whuppin's on other plantations—whup 'em half a day sometimes, gen'ly when dey tried to run away.

"We didn' have no dancin' dat I 'member, but had plen'y log rollin's. Had fiddlin', an' all would jine in singin' songs, lak, "Run nigger run, pattyrollers ketch you, run nigger run, it's breakin' days." I still fiddle dat chune[FN: tune]. Well, you see, dey jes rolled up all de old dead logs an' trees in a big pile, and burned it at night.

"I seen de Yankee sojers when dey passed our house but dey didn' bother us none. None didn' even stop in. Dey was wearin' blue jackets an' had gold buttons on caps an' jackets. But when de Confed'rate sojers come along, dey stopped an' killed a fat cow er two, an' taken de fat hoss an' lef' a lean one, an' taken ever'thing else dey seen dey wanted.

"No'm, didn' none of de slaves run off wid dem dat I knows of, an' de Yankees didn' try to bother us none. Well, afte' de War, Marse Elbert tol' us dat we was free now, an' pappy come an' got us an' taken us to live wid de cook on Mr. Elisha Bishop's place, an' he paid Mr. Barren Bishop to teach us. He taught us out of Webster's Blue Back Spellin' Book.

"My pappy, he had a stolen ejucation—'at was cause his mistress back in South Ca'Line hoped him to learn to read an' write 'fo he lef' there. You see, in dem days, it was ag'inst de law fer slaves to read.

"I was glad to be free 'cause I don't b'lieve sellin' an' whuppin' peoples is right. I certainly does think religion is a good thing, 'cause I'se a Baptist preacher right now, and I live 'bout six miles from Crystal Springs. I farm too.

United States. Work Projects Administration

Berry Smith, Ex-slave, Scott County
FEC
W.B. Allison
Rewrite, Pauline Loveless
Edited, Clara E. Stokes

BERRY SMITH
Forest, Mississippi

# BERRY SMITH

"Uncle Berry" Smith is five feet two or three inches tall. He is scrupulously neat. He is very independent for his age, which is calculated at one hundred and sixteen years. He believes the figure to be correct. His mind is amazingly clear.

"I was born an' bred in Sumpter County, Alabama, in de prairie lan', six miles from Gainesville. Dat's where I hauled cotton. It was close to Livingston, Alabama, where we lived.

"I was twelve years old when de stars fell. Dey fell late in de night an' dey lighted up de whole earth. All de chaps was a-runnin' 'roun' grabbin' for 'em, but none of us ever kotched[FN: caught] one. It's a wonder some of' em didn' hit us, but dey didn'. Dey never hit de groun' atall.

"When dey runned de Injuns out de country, me an' another chap kotched one o' dem Injun's ponies an hung him up[FN: tied him up] in de grape vines. He said it was his pony an' I said it was mine.

"Marse Bob's boy tol' us his daddy was gwine a-wh-up us for stealin' dat pony, so we hid out in de cane for two nights. Marse Bob an' his brother whupped us' til we didn' want to see no more Injuns or dey ponies, neither.

"I was born a slave to Old Marse Jim Harper an' I fell to Marse Bob. Marse Jim bought my pa an' ma from a man by de name o' Smith, an' Pa kep' de name. Dat's how come I is Berry Smith.

"Dey didn' have no schools for us an' didn' teach us nothin' but work. De bull-whip an' de paddle was all de teachin' we got. De white preachers used to preach to de Niggers sometimes in de white folks' church, but I didn' go much.

"We had fun in dem days in spite o' ever'thing. De pranks we used to play on dem paterollers! Sometimes we tied ropes 'crost de bridge an' de paterollers'd hit it an' go in de creek. Maybe we'd be fiddlin' an' dancin' on de bridge (dat was de grown folks, but de chaps 'ud come, too) an' dey'd say, 'Here come de paterollers!' Den we'd put out. If we could git to de marster's house, we was all right. Marse Bob wouldn' let no pateroller come on his place. Marse Alf wouldn', neither. Dey said it was all right if we could git home widout bein' kotched, but we have to take dat chance.

"At de Big House dey had spinnin' wheels an' a loom. Dey made all de clo'es[FN: clothes] on de place. Homespun was what dey called de goods. My ma used to spin an' weave in de loom room at de Big House.

"Dey was two plantations in de marster's lan' an' dey

worked a heap o' Niggers. I was a house boy an' didn' go to de fiel' much.

"We had overseers on de place, but dey was jus' hired men. Dey was po' white folks an' only got paid 'bout three or fo' hund'ed dollars a year.

"When we lef' Alabama we come to Mississippi. We went to de Denham place near Garlandsville. We brought eighteen Niggers. We walked a hund'ed miles an' it took five days an' nights. De women an' little chaps rid[FN: rode] on de wagons (dey had five mules to de wagon) an' de men an' de big chaps walked. My pa an' ma come along.

"We stayed on de Denham place 'bout three years. Den we moved to Homewood an' stayed five years. I hung de boards for Marse Bob's house in Homewood.

"Den we come to Forest. Dey brought all de fam'ly over here—all my brothers an' sisters. Dey was five of' em—Wash an' East is de two I 'members. All o' us b'longed to de Harper fam'ly. Marse Bob owned us. My ma an' pa both died here in Forest.

"I he'ped to build dis house for Marse Bob. I cleaned de lan' an' lef de trees where he tol' me. He lived in a little old shack whilst we built de Big House.

"Mr. M.D. Graham put up de firs' store here an' de secon' was put up by my marster.

"I worked in de fiel' some, but mos'ly I was a house servant. I used to go all over de country a-huntin' eggs an' chickens for de fam'ly on' count dey was so much comp'ny at de house.

"A heap o' white folks was good to dey Niggers, jus' as good as dey could be, but a heap of' em was mean, too. My mistis was good to us an' so was Marse Jim Harper. He wouldn' let de boys 'buse us while he lived, but when he died dey was wild an' cruel. Dey was hard taskmasters. We was fed good three times a day, but we was whupped too much. Dat got me. I couldn' stan' it. De old marster give us good dinners at Chris'mus, but de young ones stopped all dat.

"De firs' train I ever seen was in Brandon. I went dere to carry some horses for my marster. It sho' was a fine lookin' engine. I was lookin' at it out of a upstairs window an' when it whistled I'd a-jumped out dat window if Captain Harper hadn' a-grabbed me.

"I didn' see no fightin' in de war. When Gen'l Sherman come th'ough here, he come by Hillsboro. Marse Bob didn' go to de war. He 'listed[FN: enlisted], but he come right back an' went to gittin' out cross ties for de railroad. He warnt no sojer. Colonel Harper, dat was Marse Alf, he was de sojer. He warnt scared o' nothin' or nobody.

"De Yankees ask me to go to de war, but I tol' 'em, 'I aint no rabbit to live in de woods. My marster gives me three good meals a day an' a good house an' I aint a-goin'.' Marse Bob used to feed us fine an' he was good to us. He wouldn' let no overseer touch his Niggers, but he whupped us, hisse'f.

"Den de Yankees tol' me I was free, same as dey was. I come an' tol' Marse Bob I was a-goin'. He say, 'If you don't go to work, Nigger, you gwine a-git whupped.' So I run away an' hid out in de woods. De nex' day I went to

Meridian. I cooked for de sojers two months, den I come back to Forest an' worked spikin' ties for de railroad.

"I hear'd a heap of talk 'bout Jeff Davis an' Abe Lincoln, but didn' know nothin' 'bout 'em. We hear'd 'bout de Yankees fightin' to free us, but we didn' b'lieve it 'til we hear'd 'bout de fightin' at Vicksburg.

"I voted de 'publican ticket after de surrender, but I didn' bother wid no politics. I didn' want none of 'em.

"De Kloo Kluxers[FN: Ku Klux's] was bad up above here, but I never seen any. I hear'd tell of 'em whuppin' folks, but I don't know nothin' 'bout it, much.

"Mos' all de Niggers dat had good owners stayed wid 'em, but de others lef'. Some of 'em come back an' some didn'.

"I hear'd a heap o' talk 'bout ever' Nigger gittin forty acres an' a mule. Dey had us fooled up 'bout it, but I never seen nobody git nothin'.

"I hope dey won't be no more war in my time. Dat one was turrible. Dey can all go dat wants to, but I aint a goin'.

"I seen Gen'l Grant at Vicksburg after de war. (He was a little short man.) All de Niggers went dere for somethin'—me 'mongst 'em. I don't know what we went for.

"I took to steamboatin' at Vicksburg 'cause I could cut[FN: place for storage or shipment] cotton so good. (I could cut cotton now wid a cotton hook if I warnt so old.)

"I steamboated twixt New Orleans an' St. Louis on de 'Commonwealth,' a freight packet, way up yonder in

St. Louis. I don't know what country dat was in. But de rousters had a big fight one night in New Orleans, shootin' an' cuttin', so I lef'. When I got back to Vicksburg, I quit.

"I picked cotton in de Delta awhile, but de folks, white an' black, is too hard. Dey don't care 'bout nothin! I was in Greenville when de water come. I hear'd a noise like de wind an' I asked dem Niggers, 'Is dat a storm?' Dey said, 'No, dat's de river comin' th'ough an' you better come back 'fore de water ketch[FN: catch] you.' I say, 'If it ketch me it gwine a-ketch me on my way home.' I aint been back since.

"Den I come back here an' went to farmin' an' I been here ever since. I bought forty-seven acres an' a nice little house. De house burnt down, but de white folks built me a better one. Dey's good an' kin' to me. Dey say I's a good man.

"My wife was six year old at de surrender. She b'longed to Marse Alf, but we was free when we married. We had sixteen chillun. Mos' of 'em lives 'roun 'here. Some in Newton, some in Scott, an' some in Texas. My wife died two years ago las' March.

"Marse Bob died right here in dis here house. He died a po' man. If my old mistis had a-been here she wouldn' a-let' em treat him like dey done. If I'd a-been here I wouldn' a-let' em done like dat, neither.

"I been a-livin' by myse'f since my wife died. My son, Oscar, lives on de lan' an' rents it from me.

"I don't know what's gwine a-happen to de young folks now-a-days. Dey know better, but dey's wild an' don't care 'bout nothin'. I aint got no time to fool wid 'em. Looks like dey don't care 'bout workin' at nothin'.

"I been a-workin' all my life, an' I'se seen good times an' bad times. I loves to work yet. I's gwine out now soon's I git my dinner an' he'p finish pickin' dat patch o' cotton. I can pick two hund'ed pounds a day an' I's one hund'ed an' sixteen year old. I picks wid both han's an' don't have to stoop much. My back don't never ache me atall. My mammy teached me to pick cotton. She took a pole to me if I didn' do it right. I been a-pickin ever since. I'd ruther pick cotton dan eat, any day.

"But I'se seen enough. I's jus' a-waitin' for de call to meet all my folks in Heaven. Dey's a better place dan dis an' I's a-tryin' to treat ever'body right so's I can git to go to it.

"I's listenin' hard for dat call an' I know it won't be long a-comin'."

United States. Work Projects Administration

Susan Snow, Ex-slave, Lauderdale County
FEC
W.B. Allison
Rewrite, Pauline Loveless
Edited, Clara E. Stokes

SUSAN SNOW
Meridian, Mississippi

# SUSAN SNOW

"Aunt Sue" Snow, a rather small and profusely wrinkled 87-year-old ex-slave, lives in the Negro quarters of the South Side in Meridian.

In spite of her wild escapades, her reputation for honesty and reliability is high and she carries and exhibits with pride numerous letters attesting that fact.

She often finds it necessary to stand and act the story she is telling. Her memory is amazing and she turns with equal readiness to copious quotations from the Scripture and other pious observations to amusing but wholly unprintable anecdotes of her somewhat lurid past.

"I was born in Wilcox County, Alabama, in 1850. W.J. Snow was my old marster. He bought my ma from a man named Jerry Casey. Venus was her name, but dey mos'ly called her 'Venie.'

"I's workin' now for one o' my old folks. I can't work much—jus' carries things to 'er an' such. She's my old mistis' own daughter an' she's got gran'chillun grown an' married. All de chillun dat's livin' is older'n me.

"When her pa bought my mammy, I was a baby. Her pa owned a heap o' Niggers. I's de only one still hangin' aroun'.

"My ma was a black African an' she sho' was wild an' mean. She was so mean to me I couldn' b'lieve she was my mammy. Dey couldn' whup her widout tyin' her up firs'. Sometimes my marster would wait 'til de nex' day to git somebody to he'p tie her up, den he'd forgit to whup 'er. Dey used to say she was a cunger an' dey was all scared of 'er. But my ma was scared o' cungers, too.

"All de Niggers on de place was born in de fam'ly an' was kin, 'cept my ma. She tol' me how dey brought her from Africa. You know, like we say 'President' in dis country, well dey call him 'Chief' in Africa. Seem like de Chief made 'rangements wid some men an' dey had a big goober grabbin' for de young folks. Dey stole my ma an' some more an' brung 'em to dis country.

"I don't 'member nothin' 'bout havin' no pa. You know, honey, in dem days husbands an' wives didn' b'long to de same folks. My ma say her husband was so mean dat after us lef' Alabama she didn' want to marry no more.

"A man didn' git to see his wife 'cept twict a week. Dat was Wednesday an' Satu'd'y night.

"De women had to walk a chalk line. I never hear'd tell o' wives runnin' 'roun' wid other men in dem days.

"I was raised in Jasper County. Marster bought lan'

from ever'body 'roun' 'til he had a big plantation. He had Niggers, horses, mules, cows, hogs, an' chickens. He was a rich man, den.

"Ever' Nigger had a house o' his own. My ma never would have no board floor like de res' of' em, on' count she was a African—only dirt. (Dey say she was 108 year old when she died.)

"Us went to church wid de white folks if us wanted to. Dey didn' make us. I didn' go much, 'cause I didn' have 'ligion, den. Us didn' have no schoolin'. Us could go to school wid de white chillun if us wanted to, but didn' nobody teach us. I's educated, but I aint educated in de books. I's educated by de licks an' bumps I got.

"My white folks was good people an' didn' whup nobody, 'less dey needed it. Some o' de Niggers was sho' 'nough bad. Dey used to take de marster's horses out at night an' ride 'em down. One Nigger, Sam, got dat mad at a mule for grabbin' at cotton he cut his tongue out. Course, Marster whupped him, but when he went to look for 'im 'bout a hour after, he foun' 'im soun' asleep. Said he ought to kill 'im, but he didn'.

"When we was sick dey had a doctor for us jus' like dey done for deyse'ves. Dey called 'im in to 'scribe for us. I was snake-bit when I was eight year old. Dey used to be a medicine named 'lobelia.' De doctor give me dat an' whiskey. My ma carried me up to de Big House ever' mornin' an' lef' me, an' carried me home at night. Old Mis' 'ud watch over me in de day time.

"My young marster tol' me dat when I got to be ten

year old, I'd have a snake coiled up on my liver. Dat scared me mos' to death 'til I was past ten year old.

"Dey made all de Niggers' clo'es[FN: clothes] on de place. Homespun, dey called it. Dey had spinnin' wheels an' cards an' looms at de Big House. All de women spinned in de winter time.

"I never knowed what it was to wear more dan one garment, 'til I was mos' grown. I never had a pair o' shoes o' my own. Old Mis' let me wear her'n sometimes. Dey had shoes for de old folks, but not for de chillun.

"I got more whuppin's dan any other Nigger on de place, 'cause I was mean like my mammy. Always a-fightin' an' scratchin' wid white an' black. I was so bad Marster made me go look at de Niggers dey hung to see what dey done to a Nigger dat harm a white man.

"I's gwine tell dis story on myse'f. De white chillun was a-singin' dis song:

'Jeff Davis, long an' slim,
Whupped old Abe wid a hick'ry limb.

Jeff Davis is a wise man, Lincoln is a fool,
Jeff Davis rides a gray, an' Lincoln rides a mule.'

I was mad anyway, so I hopped up an' sung dis one:

'Old Gen'l Pope had a shot gun,
Filled it full o' gum,
Killed 'em as dey come.

Called a Union band,
Make de Rebels un'erstan'

To leave de lan',
Submit to Abraham.'

"Old Mis' was a-standin' right b'hin' me. She grabbed up de broom an' laid it on me. She made me submit. I caught de feathers, don't you forgit it.

"I didn' know it was wrong. I'd hear'd de Niggers sing it an' I didn' know dey was a-singin' in dey sleeves. I didn' know nothin' 'bout Abe Lincoln, but I hear'd he was a-tryin' to free de Niggers an' my mammy say she want to be free.

"De young folks used to make up a heap o' songs, den. Dey'd decompose[FN: compose] dey own songs an' sing' em. I never will forgit one song dey sung when dey buried anybody. It made Old Marster, Mistis, an' all of' em cry. Us chillun cried, too. It went like dis:

'My mother prayed in de wilderness,
In de wilderness,
In de wilderness.
My mother prayed in de wilderness.
An' den I'm a-goin' home.

Chorus:

Den I'm a-goin' home,
Den I'm a-goin' home.

We'll all make ready, Lawd,
An' den I'm a-goin' home.

She plead her cause in de wilderness,
In de wilderness,

In de wilderness.
She plead her cause in de wilderness.
An' den I'm a-goin' home.'

(Repeat chorus)

"Old Aunt Hannah fell to my marster from his daddy. She had twelve chillun a-workin' on de place. De oldes' was named Adam an' de littlest was named Eve. She had two twins what was named Rachel an' Leah. Dey nussed my mistis' two twins. Dey kep' one a-nussin' mos' all de time.

"My ma was de cause o' my marster a-firin' all de overseers. (Dey blamed ever'thing on her 'cause she was de only bought Nigger.) Marster say she was a valuable Nigger, but she was so mean he was afraid dey'd kill her. He say, 'She'll work widout no watchin' an' overseers aint nothin', nohow.'

"Dey was a white man—I aint lyin'—I know him an' I seen him. He had Nigger houn's an' he made money a-huntin' runaway Niggers. His own Niggers kilt 'im. Dey hung 'em for it. Two was his Niggers an' one b'long to somebody else.

"My young marster used to work in de fiel' wid us. He'd boss de Niggers. Dey called 'im Bud, but us all called 'im 'Babe.' Honey, I sho' did love dat boy.

"When de war come dey used to tease him an' say, 'Bud, why don't you go to de war?' Dey laughed an' teased 'im when he went. But twant no laughin' when he come home on a furlough an' went back. Dey was cryin' den. An' well dey mought[FN: might] cry, 'cause he never come back no more'. He was kilt in de war.

"Endurin' de war, de white folks made dey clo'es same as de Niggers. Old Mis' made dye an' dyed de thread. She made pretty cloth.

"My ma was de firs' to leave de plantation after de surrender. All de other Niggers had a contrac' to stay, but she didn'. She went to Newton County an' hired out. She never wanted to stay in one place, nohow. If she had a crop ha'f made an' somebody made her mad, she'd up an' leave it an' go some'r's else.

"You know, dey was mighty strict, 'bout den, wid cullud folks, an' white people, too. De Kloo Kluxes was out nights. I hear'd tell 'bout 'em whuppin' people. But dey never bothered me.

"Dey was speakers gwine aroun', tellin' de Niggers what dey was gwine a-git. Dey never got nothin' to my knowledge, 'cept de gov'ment let 'em homestead lan'. My ma homesteaded a place close to Enterprise, Scott County, but she got mad an' lef' it like she always done.

"She was a-gittin' long in years afore she got 'ligion. (She was good to me after dat.) She couldn' learn de Lawd's Prayer, but she used to pray, 'Our Father, which are in Heaven; Hallowed be Thy name. Thy mercy, Lawd, You've showed to others; That mercy show to me. Amen.' She went to res' in it, too.

"I went to Enterprise, den to Meridian, nussin' (wet-nussin' when I could) an' workin' out. I never worked in de fiel', if I could he'p it. (Old Mis' hired me out as a nuss firs' when I was eight year old.)

"When I come to Meridian, I cut loose. I's tellin' de truf! I's a woman, but I's a prodigal. I used to be a old drunkard. My white folks kep' tellin' me if I got locked up one more time dey wouldn' pay my fine. But dey done it ag'in an' ag'in.

"De Niggers called me 'Devil.' I was a devil 'til I got 'ligion. I warnt baptized 'til 1887. Den I foun' peace. I had a vision. I tol' it to a white lady an' she say, 'Susie, dat's 'ligion a-callin' you.' (But you know, honey, white folks' 'ligion aint like Niggers' 'ligion. I know a woman dat couldn' 'member de Lawd's Prayer, an' she got 'ligion out o' prayin', 'January, February, March'.) I didn' join de church 'til 1891, after I had a secon' vision. I's a member in good standin' now. I done put all my badness b'hin' me, 'cept my temper. I even got dat under more control.

"I didn' used to be scared o' cunjers. I's scared now, 'cause I had it done to me. I want to bed well an' healthy an' de nex' nornin' I couldn' git up atall. I's tellin de truf. A cullud man done it. He was a crippled man, an' mean as he could be. I was good to him, too. He tol' me' bout it, hisse'f:

"'He went to de graveyard an' got some o' de meanes' dirt he could fin' (I don't know how he knowed which was de meanes' grave) an' put it under my doorsill.' He sho' fix' me. I ask him how come he done it to me an' I been so good to him. He smile kinda tickle-lak an' say, 'It's a good thing you was good to me, 'cause, if you hadn' a-been you'd a-been dead an' in yo' grave by now.'

"I aint got nary soul what's kin to me dat I knows of. I don't want none of 'em comin' to me now an' a-sayin', 'Don't you 'member yo' own cousin?' My white folks he'p me when I needs it.

"Dese young folks. Shucks! Chile, dey's worse'n what I was, only dey's more slyer. Dat's all.

"I's glad I'se got 'ligion, 'cause when I dies I's gwine to de 'Good Place.'"

United States. Work Projects Administration

Isaac Stier, Ex-slave, Lauderdale County
FEC
Edith Wyatt Moore
Rewrite, Pauline Loveless
Edited, Clara E. Stokes

ISAAC STIER
Natchez, Mississippi

# ISAAC STIER

"Miss, my name is Isaac Stier, but folks calls me 'Ike.' I was named by my pappy's young Marster an' I aint never tol' nobody all o' dat name. It's got twenty-two letters in it. It's wrote but in de fam'ly Bible. Dat's how I knows I'll be one hund'ed years old if I lives 'til de turn o' de year. I was born in Jefferson County 'tween Hamburg an' Union Church. De plantation joined de Whitney place an' de Montgomery place, too. I b'longed to Marse Jeems Stowers. I don't rightly 'member how many acres my Marster owned, but 'twas a big plantation wid eighty or ninety head o' grown folks workin' it. No tellin' how many little black folks dey was.

"My mammy was Ellen Stier an' my pappy was Jordon Stier. He was bought to dis country by a slave dealer from Nashville, Tennessee. Dey traveled all de way through de Injun Country on afoot. Dey come on dat Trace road. Twant nothin' but a Injun Trail.

"When dey got to Natchez de slaves was put in de pen 'tached to de slave markets. It stood at de forks o'

St. Catherine Street an' de Liberty road. Here dey was fed an' washed an' rubbed down lak race hosses. Den dey was dressed up an' put through de paces dat would show off dey muscles. My pappy was sol' as a twelve year old, but he always said he was nigher twenty.

"De firs' man what bought him was a preacher, but he only kep' 'im a little while. Den he was sol' to Mr. Preacher Robinson. He was a Methodis'.

"De slaves was well treated when dey got sick. My Marster had a standin' doctor what he paid by de year. Dey was a horspital building near de quarters an' a good old granny woman to nuss de sick. Dey was five or six beds in a room. One room was for mens an' one for wimmins. Us doctor was name Richardson an' he tended us long after de war. He sho' was a gent'man an' a powerful good doctor.

"Us had a overseer on de place, but he warnt mean lak I'se heard o' other folks havin'. He was Mr. William Robinson. He was good to ever'body, both white an' cullud. Folks didn' min' workin' for him, 'cause, he spoke kin'. But dey dassen' sass 'im. He was poor. My pappy b'longed to his pa, Mr. John Robinson. Dat was a nice fam'ly wid sho' 'nough 'ligion. Whilst dey warnt rich, dey had learnin'.

"As a little tike I wore long slip-lak shirts. When dey sont me to town I put on britches an' stuffed de tail o' my slip in 'em so's it pass' for a shirt. I always lived in de Big House an' played wid de white chillun. I sorta looked after' em. I carried 'em to school. Den whilst dey was in school I roamed de woods a-huntin'. Sometimes I'd git a big bag o' game, mos'ly used to feed de slaves.

"My mistis was Miss Sarah Stowers an' she teached me how to read. She teached me how to be mannerly, too. On church days I driv'[FN: drove] de carriage. I was proud to take my folks to meetin'. I always set in de back pew an' heard de preachin' de same as dey did.

"De bes' times I can 'member always come 'roun' de Fourth o' July. Dat was always de beginnin' o' camp-meetin'. Aint nothin' lak dat in dese days.

"Ever'body what had any standin' went. Dey cooked up whole trunks full o' good things t'eat an' driv' over to de camp groun's. De preacher had a big pavilion covered wid sweet-gum branches an' carpeted wid sawdust. Folks had wagons wid hay an' quilts whar de men-folks slep'. De ladies slep' in little log houses an' dey took dey feather beds wid' em. I always driv' de carriage for my white folks. Whilst dey was a-worshipin' I'd slip 'roun' an' tas' out o' dey basket. Ever' day I'd eat 'til I was ready to bus'. One day I got so sick I thought I'd pop wide open. I crawled down to de spring an' washed my face in col' water, but I kep' gittin' worse an' worse. Den somebody called out: 'Captain Stier, yo' Nigger's a-dyin'!' My marster called de doctor. He sho' was shamed in public, 'cause, he knowed pos'tive I'd been a-pilferin' in dem baskets. Dem sho' was good old days. I'd love to live' em over ag'in.

"Us slaves mos'ly sung hymns an' sa'ms.[TR: footnote indicated but none found] But I' member one song' bout a frog pond an' one 'bout 'Jump, Mr. Toad.' I's too wordless to sing 'em now, but dey was funny. Us danced plenty, too. Some o' de men clogged an' pidgeoned, but when us had dances dey was real cotillions, lak de white folks had. Dey was always a fiddler an', on Chris'mus an' other holidays, de slaves was' lowed to' vite dey sweethearts from other plantations. I use to call out de figgers: 'Ladies, sasshay, Gents to de lef, now all swing.' Ever'body lak my calls an' de dancers sho' moved smooth an' pretty. Long after de war was over de white folks would 'gage me to come' roun' wid de band an' call de figgers at all de big dances. Dey always paid me well.

"Old Mis' 'ud let us cook a gran' supper an' Marse 'ud slip us some likker. Dem suppers was de bes' I ever et. Sometimes dey'd be wil' turkey, fried fish, hot corn pone, fresh pork ham, baked yams, chitlins, pop corn, apple pie, pound cake, raisins, an' coffee. Law, Miss! de folks now-a-days don't know nothin' 'bout good eatin', nowhow.

"When de big war broke out I sho' stuck by my marster. I fit[FN: fought] de Yankees same as he did. I went in de battles 'long side o' him an' both fit under Marse Robert E. Lee. I reckon ever'body has heard 'bout him. I seen more folks dan anybody could count. Heaps of 'em was all tore to pieces an' cryin' to God to let 'em die. I toted water to dem in blue de same as dem in gray. Folks wouldn' b'lieve de truf if I was to tell all I knows 'bout dem ungodly times.

"Fore de war I never knowed what it was to go empty. My marster sho' set a fine table an' fed his people de highes'. De hongriest I ever been was at de Siege o' Vicksburg. Dat was a time I'd lak to forget. De folks et up all de cats an' dogs an' den went to devourin' de mules an' hosses. Even de wimmin an' little chillun was a-starvin'. Dey stummicks was stickin' to dey backbones. Us Niggers was sufferin' so us took de sweaty hoss blankets an' soaked 'em in mudholes where de hosses tromped. Den us wrung' em out in buckets an' drunk dat dirty water for pot-likker. It tasted kinda salty an' was strength'nin', lak weak soup.

"I tell you, dem Yankees took us by starvation. Twant a fair fight. Dey called it a vict'ry an' bragged 'bout Vicksburg a-fallin', but hongry folks aint got no fight lef' in 'em. Us folks was starved into surrenderin'.

"De slaves spected a heap from freedon dey didn' git. Dey was led to b'lieve dey would have a easy time—go places widout passes—an have plenty o' spendin' money. But dey sho' got fooled. Mos' of 'em didn' fin' deyse'ves no better off. Pussonally, I had a harder time after de war dan I did endurin' slav'ry.

"De Yankees passed as us frien's. Dey made big promises, but dey was poor reliance. Some of' em meant well towards us, but dey was mistol' 'bout a heap o' things. Dey promised us a mule an' forty acres o' lan'. Us aint seen no mule yet. Us got de lan' all right, but twant no service. Fac' is, 'twas way over in a territory where nothin' 'ud grow. I didn' know nothin' 'bout farmin', nowhow, I'd always been a coachman an' play companion to de white chillun.

"De war was over in May 1865, but I was captured at Vicksburg an' hel' in jail 'til I 'greed to take up arms wid de Nawth. I figgered dat was 'bout all I could do, 'cause dey warnt but one war at Vicksburg an' dat was over. I was all de time hopin' I could slip off an' work my way back home, but de Yankees didn' turn me loose 'til 1866.

"Den I worked in a saloon in St. Louis. Dat was 'bout all I knowed to do. All de time I was a-cravin' to come back to Mississippi. It sho' suits my tas' better'n anywhere I'se ever been.

"When I landed back home my white folks welcome me. After awhile I married a gal what was real smart 'bout farmin' an' chicken raisin'. So us share-cropped an' raised a fam'ly. Somehow us always scrapped along. Sometimes it was by de hardes', but us always had plenty t'eat.

"All de cullud folks what lived to git back home took to de lan' ag'in. If dey marster was dead dey went to his frien's an' offered to share-crop. Dey was all plumb sick o' war. Is sho' is ongodly business. I never will forgit de fearsome sight o' seein' men die 'fore dey time. War sho' is de debbil's own work.

"De Klu Klux Klan didn' bother me none. Course, I was feared of' em at firs', but I soon learnt dat long as I b'haved myse'f an' tended my business dey warnt after me. Dey sho' disastered dem what meddled wid de white folks. Nobody but a smart Alec would a-done dat. Only Niggers huntin' trouble mixed into white folks bus'ness. Onct or twict I seen Klu Klux's ridin' by, but dey always traveled fas' an' I kep' my mouf[FN: mouth] shut.

"After de war my marster come back home. De fences was gone, de cattle was gone, de money an' de Niggers was gone, too. On top o' all dat de whole country was over-run an' plumb took over by white trash. It was cautious times.

"After awhile, robbers an' low down trash got to wearin' robes an' pretendin' dey was Klu Klux's. Folks called dem de 'white caps.' Dey was vicious, an' us was more scared of 'em dan us'd ever been o' de Klan. When dey got likkered up de debbil sho' was turnt loose.

"Mr. Jefferson Davis was pretty good' bout some things. But if he hadn' a-been mulish he could-a 'cepted de proposition Mr. Abe Lincum made 'im. Den slav'ry would-a lasted always. But he flew into a huff an' swore dat he'd whip de Yankees wid corn stalks. Dat made Mr. Lincum mad, so he sot about to free de slaves.

"Mr. Lincum was a good man, but dey tells me he was poor an' never cut much figger in his clothes. Dat's why he never did un'erstan' how us felt' bout us white folks. It takes de quality to un'erstan' such things.

"Right now, I loves my marster an' his wife in de grave. Dey raised me an' showed me kindness all dey lives. I was proud of 'em. At de present time I's under treatment o' young Dr. Stowers, my marster's gran'chil'. I trusts him an' he is sho' good to me.

"I rents a place on Providence Plantation 'bout three miles south o' Natchez. De trip to Natchez in a rickety old wagon is mos' too much in de hot weather. My heart's mos' wore out. I can't las' long, 'cause I's had a heap sposure[FN: exposure].

"I's jus' a bag o' bones now, but onct I stood nearly six feet in my stockings an' weighed 'bout one hundred an' eighty pounds. I was well muscled, too. Now I's gittin' kinda gray an' gittin' bald at de same time. Black folks lak me don't hardly ever git bald.

"I's gittin' real feeble. De doctor say I got a bad heart. Sometimes I jus' has to set on de curb an' res' myse'f a spell. I gits kinda windless when I thinks 'bout all I been through.

"My wife is been dead 'bout seventeen years an' my chillun is so scattered dat I don't know where dey is. De folks I stays wid is powerful good to me an' sees after me same as dey was my own. I reckon I don't need nothin else.

"Dis generation aint got much sense. Dey's tryin' to git somewheres too fas'. None of 'em is sat'fied wid plain livin'. Dey wants too much.

"Nobody needs more dan dey can use, nohow."

**JANE SUTTON**
Gulfport, Mississippi

# JANE SUTTON

Jane Sutton, ex-slave, is 84 years old. She is 5 feet, 6 inches tall and weighs 130 pounds. She is what the Negroes themselves call a "brown-skin."

"I was born in Simpson County, near old Westville, on a big farm what b'long to Marse Jack Berry. I was 12 years old when de surrender come, so my ole Mis' say. Her name was 'Mis Ailsey an' all us cullud folks call her 'Ole Mi's. She an' Old Marster had twelve chillun: Marthy, 'Lizabeth, Flavilia, Mary, Jack, Bill, Denson, Pink, Tally, Thomas, Albert, and Frank.

"My pappy's name was Steve Hutchins. He b'long to de Hutchins what live down near Silver Creek. He jus' come on Satu'd'y night an' us don' see much of 'im. Us call him 'dat man.' Mammy tol' us to be more 'spectful to 'im 'cause he was us daddy, but us aint care nothin' 'bout 'im. He aint never brung us no candy or nothin'.

"My mammy was name Lucy Berry. She always go by de white folks name what she live wid. She aint never marry. She had fo' boys an' three girls. Dey was name Delia, Sarah, Ella, Nathan, Isom, Anderson, an' Pleas. She work in de fiel' an Old Marster say she's de only woman on de place what could plow lak a man.

"I 'members my gran'ma, too. Us always call her

'Granny.' She say dey stole her back in Virginny an' brung 'er to Mississippi an' sol' her to Marse Berry. Her name was Hannah. She was my mammy's Mammy. I don' 'member nothin' 'bout my pappy's folks 'cause I never seen none of' em.

"Old Marster was a rich man for dat day. He had a sawmill, a cotton gin, an' a gris' mill. Us always had plenty t'eat an' wear. Dey spun an' weaved dey own cloth an' made us clo'es out-a it.

"I can jus' see de white folk's house now. It was a big house, nice an' clean, but twant painted. It had a row o' rooms 'cross dis way an' a-nother row dat way wid a hall between. Dey had plenty o' rooms for all dem boys an' gals. Some of 'em was 'bout grown. De quarters[FN: slave quarters] was in de back o' de house. De cook's house was closes' to de Big House, den nex' was Granny's house where us stayed. Den come a long row way down to de back fence.

"Dey didn' have no overseer or driver. Dey was 'nough o' dem boys to look after de work an' Old Marster say he don' need no overseer to look after his slaves.

"My white folks was all Baptis' an' dey made us go to church, too. De church was called de Strong River Church. Dey had big baptisin's. I 'members when I joined de church. De white folks preacher baptised us in de creek what run from Marse Berry's mill pond. I was dressed up in a white lowell slip. When us dress' up in Sund'y clo'es us had caliker[FN: calico] dresses. Dey sho' was pretty. I 'members a dress now dat Old Marster bought for my granny. It was white an' yaller, an' it was de prettiest thing I ever seen.

"Us white folks was good to us. Dey warnt always a-beatin' an' a-knockin' us 'roun'. De truf is you couldn' fin' a scar on nary one o' us. 'Course, some times dey whup us, but dey didn' gash us lak some o' de old marsters did dey Niggers.

"When Old Marster died I didn' know nothin' bout him bein' sick. He took a cramp colic in de night an' was dead 'fore mornin'. I hear somebody a-cryin' at de Big House an' Granny tol' us dat Old Marster done die in de night. Dey had a big fun'al an' all de folks come. De men carried him to de graveyard by de church. Dey didn' have no hearses dem days. Twant far to de graveyard so dey jus' toted de coffin to whar dey buried 'im. Dey put flowers in cups an' vases on de grave, so's dey wouldn' wilt.

"Us was all sorry when Old Marster died, I cried 'cause I said, 'Now us won' git no more candy.' He used to bring us candy whan he went to town. Us'd be lookin' for 'im when he come home. He'd say, 'Whars all my little Niggers?' Den us'd come a-runnin' an' he'd han' it to us out-a his saddle bags. It was mos'ly good stick candy.

"I 'members de paterollers. Whenever de cullud folks would slip off an' have dey frolics dout gittin' a pass from Old Marster de paterollers would come. Lots-a time dey'd come while us was a-dancin' an' a-havin' a big time. Dem paterollers would swarm in de room lak a lot o' bees. Fore anybody knowed it, dey'd begin grabbing at de mens. If dey didn' have dey pass wid 'em dey took 'em down in de woods an' whup 'em for runnin' off wid out asking dey white folks. Dey didn' bother de wimnins much. De wimmins mos' always got away while dey was catchin' de mens.

"Onct I slipped off wid another gal an' went to a party dout asking Old Mis'. When dem Night Riders come dat night, de Niggers was a-runnin' an' a-dodgin' an' a-jumpin' out-a winders lak dey was scairt to death. I runs too, me an' dat other gal. I fell down an' tore my dress, but I warnt studyin' dat dress. I knows dat dem white folks had dat strap an' I's gittin' 'way fas' as I could.

"When Miss 'Lizabeth got married to Mr. Ras Laird, dey had a big weddin' an' all dey folks come to see 'em married. Den dey went to live in Rankin County an' took me wid 'em. Old Marster had give me to Miss 'Lizabeth.

"I 'members when de Yankees come to de house. Us heard dey was comin', so us hid all de hams an' shoulders up in de lof' o' de Big House. Dey didn' git much. Dey was so mad dey jus' tore up some of Old Mis' clo'es what was in de wardrobe. Us was sho' scairt of 'em.

"I 'members dey promise to give de cullud folks all kin' o' things. Dey never give 'em nothin' dat I know's about. Us was jus' turnt loose to scratch for us ownse'ves. Us was glad to stay on wid de white folks, 'cause dey was de bes' frien's us had. I don' know nobody what got a thing 'cept what Old Marster an' Old Mis' give 'em.

"After freedom I went back to 'Old Mis'. I walked all de way back from Rankin County. It was a long way, but I wanted to see Old Mis' an' my Mammy an' my brothers an' sisters.

"When de surrender come by pappy come to git me. I didn' wan'-a go. I tol' 'im I's gwine stay wid Old Mis'. So he goes an' gits de sheriff an' takes me anyway. I runned away twict an' come back to Old Mis'. He whupped me de firs' time, but de nex' time I hid from him an' he couldn' catch me. He went back home an' 'lemme 'lone. Den I went wid my mammy to live wid Marse Tally Berry. He was one of Old Marster's sons. Dey used to come an' tell me dat dat old Nigger was gwine kill me if I didn' come wid him. But I jus' stayed hid out till he went away.

"I spec' all my white folks is dead now. I wish I could go back to 'em now. Dey help me. Dey was good to us after de War was over. Dis one would want me to live wid dem, den de other one would want me to live wid dem. Sometimes I quit one an' go live wid de other one. All of 'em sho' did treat me good. I's havin' a heap harder time now dan I ever had in slav'ry times. I sho' is.

"Dey raised de young folks better dem days. Dey learnt 'em to work. Dey didn' min' work. Today dey don' care 'bout nothin' but havin' a good time. Dey ain' studyin' 'bout no hereafter, neither.

"De Relief give me a little somethin' t'eat an' wear one time, but dey aint never give me no money. I's old an' needy, but I's trustin' de Lord an' de good white folks to he'p me now. All de white folks I used to work for has moved away from town now. I don' have nobody to look to but my daughter. She looks after me de bes' she can. Dey is some neighbor wimmins dat comes an' sets wid me sometimes.

"I's gittin' deaf an' I aint got a tooth lef' in my head. I's too feeble to he'p make a livin', but maybe I'll git dat Old Age Pension 'fore I die."

United States. Work Projects Administration

**Mississippi Federal Writers**
**Slave Autobiographies**

[MOLLIE WILLIAMS
Terry, Mississippi]

# MOLLIE WILLIAMS

Mollie Williams, who lives two miles west of Terry, Miss., tells her story:

"Iffen I lives' til nex' September 15, I'll be eighty fo'! I was born 'bout three miles frum Utica on de

Newsome place. Me an' brudder Hamp b'longed to Marse George Newsome. Marse George was named afte' George Washington up in Virginny whar he come frum. Miss Margurite was our mistiss. My mammy? Well, I'll have to tell you now 'bout her.

"You see, Marse George come off down here frum Virginny lak young folks venturin' 'bout, an' mar'ied Mis' Margurite an' wanted to start up livin' right over thar near Utica whar I was born. But Marse George was po', an' he sho' foun' out ye can't make no crop wid'out'n a start of darkies, so he writ home to Virginny fer to git some darkies. All dey sont him was fo' mens an' old Aunt Harriet fer to cook.

"One day Marse George an' his Uncle, Mr. John Davenport—now thar was a rich man fer ye, why, he had two carri'ge drivers—dey rid over to Grand Gulf whar dey was a sellin' slabes offen de block an' Mr. John tol' Marse George to pick hisself out a pair of darkies to mate so's he could git hisself a start of darkies fer to chop his cotton an' like. So Marse George pick out my pappy fust. My pappy come frum North Ca'lina. Den he seen my mammy an' she was big an' strengthy an' he wanted her pow'ful bad. But lak I tol' you, he didn' have 'nough money to buy 'em both, so his Uncle John say he'd buy mammy an' den he would loan her over to Marse George fer pappy. An' de fust chile would be Mr. John's, an' de secon' Marse George's, an' likewise. Mammy was a Missourian name Marylin Napier Davenpo't. An' pappy was name Martin Newsome.

"Darkies libed in li'l old log houses wid dirt chimbleys. Dat is, de rest of de darkies did. Dey kep' me up in de Big House, bein' mammyless lak. Mos'ly I slep' in de trun'le bed wid Miss Mary Jane till I got so bad dey had to mek a pallet on de flo' fer me. Dey was Mr. Bryant, Mr. A.D., Miss Martha, Miss Ann, Miss Helen, Miss Mary Jane, an' Mr. George, all b'longin' to Marse George an' Miss Margurite.

"Mammy was a fiel' han'. She could plow an' wuk in de fiel's jes' lak a man, an' my pappy, he done de same. Mammy, she hated house wuk—lak me. I jes natu'lly loves to be out runnin' roun' in de fiel's an' 'bout. I neber lak'd to do wuk roun' de house none t'all.

"We wo' lowell clo'es an' brass toed brogans. Miss Margurite made our dresses an' lak, an' afte' Aunt Harriet died, she done de cookin' too fer all de slabes an' de fambly. She fix up dinner fer de fiel' han's, an' I taken it to 'em. Marse George had old powder horn he blowed mornin's far to git de darkies up 'fo day good, an' dey come in 'bout sundown.

"We growed corn an' taters an' cotton plentiful, an' we had gran' orchids[FN: orchids] an' penders[FN: peanuts]. Den, sheeps an' hogs an' cows an' lak.

"Miss Margurite had a piany, a 'cordian, a flutena, an' a fiddle. She could play a fiddle good as a man. Law, I heerd many as three fiddles goin' in dat house many a time, an' I kin jes see her li'l old fair han's now, playin' jes as fast as lightnin' a chune[FN: tune] 'bout

**[HW: Song]**

'My father he cried, my mother she cried,
I wasn' cut out fer de army.
O, Capt'in Gink, my hoss me think,

But feed his hoss on co'n an' beans
An s'port de gals by any means!
'Cause I'm a Capt'in in de army.'

"All us chullun begged ter play dat an' we all sing an' dance—great goodness!

"One song I 'member mammy singin':

**[HW: Song]**

'Let me nigh, by my cry,
Give me Jesus.
You may have all dis world,
But give me Jesus.'

"Singin' an' shoutin', she had 'ligion all right. She b'longed to Old Farrett back in Missouri.

"We didn' git sick much, but mammy made yeller top tea[FN: dog fennel] fer chills an' fever an' give us. Den iffen it didn' do no good, Miss Margurite called fer Dr. Hunt lak she done when her own chullun got sick.

"None of de darkies on dat place could read an' write. Guess Miss Helen an' Miss Ann would'a learned me, but I was jes so bad an' didn' lak to set still no longer'n I had to.

"I seen plenty of darkies whupped. Marse George buckled my mammy down an' whupped her 'cause she run off. Once when Marse George seen pappy stealin' a bucket of 'lasses an' totin' it to a gal on 'nother place, he whupped him but didn' stake him down. Pappy tol' him to whup him but not to stake him—he'd stan' fer it wid'out de stakin'—so I 'member he looked jes lak he was jumpin' a rope an' hollerin', 'Pray Marser', ever time de strop hit 'im.

"I heered 'bout some people whut nailed de darkies years[FN: ears] to a tree an' beat' em but I neber seen none whupped dat way.

"I neber got no whuppins frum Marse George 'cause he didn' whup de chulluns none. Li'l darky chullun played 'long wid white chullun. Iffen de old house is still thar I 'spec you kin fin' mud cakes up under de house whut we made out'n eggs we stole frum de hen nests. Den we milked jes anybody's cows we could ketch, an' churned it. We's all time in ter some mischief.

"Thar was plenty dancin' 'mong'st darkies on Marse George's place an' on ones nearby. Dey danced reels an' lak in de moonlight:

**[HW: Songs]**

'Mamma's got de whoopin' cough,
Daddy's got de measles,
Dat's whar de money goes,
Pop goes de weasel.'


'Buffalo gals, can't you come out tonight,
Come out tonight, an' dance by de light of de moon?'


'Gennie, put de kettle on,
Sallie, boil de water strong,
Gennie, put de kittle on
An' le's have tea!'

'Run tell Coleman,
Run tell everbody
Dat de niggers is arisin'!'

'Run nigger run, de patterrollers ketch you—
Run nigger run, fer hits almos' day,
De nigger run; de nigger flew; de nigger los'
His big old shoe.'

"When de War come, Marse George went to fight back in Virginny. Us all thought de Yankees was some kin' of debils an' we was skeered to death of 'em.

"One day Miss Mary Jane, Helen, an' me was playin' an' we seen mens all dressed in blue coats wid brass buttons on dey bosoms ridin' on big fine hosses, drive right up to our po'ch an' say to Aunt Dalia whar she was sweepin':

"'Good morning, Madam, no men's about?'

"When she tol' 'em wa'nt no mens 'bout, day ax fer de keys to de smokehouse an' went out an' hap'ed deyse'ves an' loaded dey wagons. Den dey went out in de pasture 'mongst de sheeps an' killed off some of dem. Nex' dey went in de buggy house an' all together shuck down de carri'ge so we neber could use hit no mo'. Yessum, dey done right smart of mischief 'roun' thar.

"Some of de darkies went off wid de Yankees. My brudder Howard did, an' we ain't heerd tell of him since. I'll tell you 'bout it. You see, Mr. Davenpo't owned him an' when he heard 'bout da Yankees comin' dis way, he sont his white driver an' Howard in de carri'ge wid all his valuables to de swamp to hide, an' while dey was thar de white driver, he went off to sleep an' Howard was prowlin' 'roun' an' we all jes reckin he went on off wid de Yankees.

**[HW: Superstition]**

"You mean hoo doo? Dat's whut ma pappy done to my mammy. You see, dey was allus fussin' 'bout fust one thing, den 'nother, an' mammy got mad 'caus'n pappy slipped her clo'es out'n her ches' an' taken over to de other gals fer to dance in, an' when he brung' em back mammy would see finger prints on' em whar he been turnin' 'em 'roun' an' she sho' be mad an' fight him. She could lick him too caus'n she was bigger. One day pappy come in an' say to mammy:

"'Does you want to be bigger an' stronger dan whut you already is?' An' mammy say she did. So nex' day he brung her a li'l bottle of somethin' blood red wid somethin' looked like a gourd seed in de middle of it, an' he tol' her to drink hit iffen she want to be real strong. Frum de fust drink she fell off. Place of walkin' off, she jes stumbled an' got wo'ser an' wo'ser till she plum los' her min'. Fer a long time, dey had to tie her to a tree. Den afte' de War, she lef Mr. Davenpo't's an' jes traveled 'bout over de country. I stayed on wid Miss Margurite he'pin' her jes lak I'd been doin'. One day mammy come afte' me an' I run an' hid under a pile of quilts an' laked to smothered to death waitin' fer her to go on off.

"Nex' time she come, she brung a written letter to

Miss Margurite frum de Free Man's Board an' taken me wid her. We jes went frum place to place 'til I got mar'ied an' settled down fer myself. I had three chullun, but ain't none livin' now."

**Mississippi Federal Writers
Slave Autobiographies**

[TOM WILSON
near New Zion Church, Mississippi]

# TOM WILSON

"My name is Tom Wilson an' I'se eighty fo' years old. My mammy was name Ca'line an' my pappy was Jeff Wilson. Us lived right out on de old Jim Wilson place, right by New Zion Chu'ch. I lives thar now—owns me a plot of groun' an' farms.

"Well, us b'longed to Marse Jim an' Miss Nancy Wilson. I was born right out thar, but my mammy was brung down frum Ten'see. She come by heir to Marse Jim but 'fo that her was sol' for ten hun'erd dollars. My mammy was a big sportly woman an' brung a lot er money an' my pappy, he brung nine hun'erd. Marse Jim bought him offen de block, but I don't know jes whar frum. I jes 'members 'bout hearin' him tell 'bout bein' sol'.

"Bofe of dem was fiel' han's. Law, mammy could plow jes lak a man all day long; den milk twen'y head er cows afte' she quit de fiel' at night.

"De Big House was made out'n logs an' reckin hit had 'bout seben er eight rooms in hit, an' de kitchen sot a piece frum de mainest house. Thar was one brick chimbly an' one dirt one to hit, an' a great big wide po'ch 'cross de front of de house. I 'member Mis Nancy an' white folks 'ud set out thar of an evenin' an' mek us li'l cullud chullun dance an' sing an' cut capers fer to 'muse 'em. Den dey had a trough, built 'bout lak a pig trough, an' dey would mek de cook bake a gre't big slab er co'n bread an' put hit in de trough an' po' milk or lasses over hit, an' tu'n us li'l cullud chullun loose on hit. An' I'se tell'n y' as much of hit went in our hair an' eyes an' years[FN: ears] as went in our moufs[FN: mouths].

"I reckin thar was' bout two er three hun'erd acres in Marse Jim's place. Us raised cotton, taters, an' hogs. No'm, slaves didn' have no plots er dey own. Marse Jim give us our rashins' every week. Well, mos' er de cullud people 'ud cook dey victuals over de fire place in dey own houses. Us sho' did have 'possum an' taters.

"My mammy wuked in de loom room at night by light

of a pine knot. In de Big House dey had taller[FN: tallow] can'les 'cause I 'member my mammy moulded 'em. No'm, de spinnin' wheels was kep' in de kitchen of de Big House. Hit had a dirt flo'. Us jes wo' li'l old suits made out'n lowell cloth whut mammy wove on de loom. I doan 'member wearin' no shoes.

"I jes played roun' 'bout de place an' he'ped wid de cleanin' up an' dish washin'. Kinder house boy, I was.

### [HW: Medicine]

"When us got sick, mammy made us pills out'n herbs. She taken May apple roots an' boiled hit down to a syrup; den she let dat, dry out an' rolled hit inter pills. Day sho' was fin' fo' mos' anything we might have.

"Chris'mus was a mighty glad time fo' us. Yessum, us got extra rashins' an' had time off ter play an' kick our heels. Gen'ly[FN: generally] had 'bout a week off. Tell you what Marse Jim 'ud do when Chris'mus come 'roun'. He'd sen' one of da cullud mans out to git a log an' say, 'Now long as dis log burn, y'all kin have off'n wuk'. Co'se us'd hunt de bigges' gum log an' den soak hit in de stream so hit wud burn on a long time. Dey'd put hit on back er de fire an' hit wud las' mos' a week.

"Couldn' none of us read or write, an' us wa'nt neber learned 'til afte' us was set free. Den some went to li'l schools fer da cullud people.

"I sho' has seen m' mammy an' lots mo' git whuppins. Marse Jim, he had a strop er leather stuck in de slit end of a staff, an' he sho' did whup 'em layed 'cross a barrel. Once' m' pappy run away an' Marse Jim got de blood houn's afte' him, an' catched him up 'fo he could git fur, an' dat day he lay him 'cross de barrel, an' whupped him frum sun up til sun down. When he quit off, m' pappy couldn' talk no more'n a whisper sca'cely.

"Pattyrollers, I heard of 'em allright 'cause dey sho' would git you iffen y' went abroad widout a pass frum Marse Jim.

"One day us li'l cullud chullun was frollicin' out in de front yard an' Mis' Nancy an' some mo' was settin' on de po'ch an' all of a sudden I see somebuddy comin' down de road an' I says 'Look, whut's dat?'

"An' white folks run to de woods an' hid out caze dey seen hit was Calv'ry 'bout a mile long comin' down de road. Sojer rid right up to me an' stuck his bay'net at me an' says, 'Boy, whar de tater house?' An' I sho' did show him whar 'twas. Dem sojers sho' was starved. Dey take thirty tater punks, fifteen er twenty chickens, and five hams. Den dey went in de smoke house an' grabbed off five er ten poun's er sausage, middlln's, and sides. Dey take 'nough grub to load three wagons an' take hit over to New Zion Church 'bout er mile frum us. An' right thar dey camped that night.

"That was afte' de Siege er Vicksburg. Marse Jim didn' keer, but he sent us ober nex' mo'nin' to git de leavin's, an' thar was a wagon load er jes de leavin's.

"I 'members when us was sot free allright. 'Twas in de middle of da winter y' know, an' Marse Jim was so mad 'bout hit he went off down to a li'l stream or water an' broke de ice an' jumped in, an' he died 'bout two weeks afte' of de pewmonia[FN: pneumonia].

"I was glad to git m' freedom 'cause I got out'n frum under dem whuppins.

"Afte' dat us bought lan' frum de Wilsons whut was lef' an' I been a fa'min' thar ever since."

United States. Work Projects Administration

**Mississippi Federal Writers
Slave Autobiographies**

CLARA C. YOUNG
Monroe County, Mississippi

# CLARA C. YOUNG

Clara G. Young, ex-slave, Monroe County, is approximately 95 years old, about five feet two inches tall, and weighs 105 pounds. She is a frail, dark skinned Negro, with the typical broad nose and the large mouth of the southern Negro. Her physical condition is especially good for a woman of her age. She is very talkative at times, but her memory appears to come and go, so that she has to be prompted at intervals in her story-telling by her daughter or granddaughter, with whom she lives. Familiarly known as "Aunt Classie," she is very proud of her age and more especially of her long line of descendants.

"Law, Miss, I doan know when I was born, but I do know dat I'se sebenteen years old when I was fust sol'. Dey put me an' my brudder up on de auction block at de same time. He brung $1400 but I dis'members zactly what dey paid far me. Wa'nt dat much, tho', fer big strong mans brung mo' dan wimmens an' gals."

Long pauses accentuated the quavery voice of the old Negro, whose head resembled a nappy patch of cotton, and who was so enthusiastic over reminiscing about the days when she was young and carefree.

"I was born in Huntsville, Alabamy, an' my mammy an' pappy was name Silby an' Sharper Conley. Dey tuk de las' name frum de old marster dat owned 'em. I lived dar wid 'em 'til de chullun drew dey parts an' us was 'vided out. While I was wid old marster, he let Miss Rachel—dat was his wife—have me fer de house. She larned me how to cook an' wait on de table, an' I declar', she call me her ver' smartest gal! Sometimes, tho', I wouldn' come right quick lak when she ring de bell fer me, an' she'd start ringin' it harder an' harder. I knowed den she was mad. When I'd get dar, she'd fuss at me an' tu'n my dress up an' whup me—not hard 'cause she wa'nt so strong—but I'd holler some!

"Dey had a nigger woman to teach all de house darkies how to read an' write an' I larned how to sign my name an' got as fur as b-a-k-e-r in de Blue Back Speller.

"Marse Conley an' Miss Rachel had fo' chullun, Miss Mary, Miss Alice, Miss Willie, an' Marse Andrew, an' when de time come, dey give me to Marse Andrew. He car'ied me an' de rest out to Texas whar he thought he would go an' git rich. We neber stayed long, tho', fer lots of de niggers runned 'way to de Free State an' Marse Andrew didn' lak dat.

**[HW: Pre-War Days]**

"It was when he brought us back to Huntsville dat I was sol'. All de white folks was a gittin' scared dey was gwineter lose dey slaves an' dere was a pow'ful lot er nigger sellin' goin' on den. Marse Ewing bought me frum him an' car'ied me to his plantation near Aberdeen, Mississippi. Den I started to workin' in de fiel' wid de rest of de hands. De oberseer dat we had was right mean to us when we didn' work our rows as fas' as de others, an' sometime he whup us, wimmen an' all. When he did dat some of us most nigh allus tell de marster an' he would jump on de oberseer an' tell him to lay off de wimmen an' chullun. Dey was allus sort of thoughtful of us an' we loved old marster.

"I heerd tell one time, tho', of de hired man (he was a nigger) an' de oberseer whuppin' one of my cousins 'til she bled; she was jes' sebenteen years old an' was in de fambly way fer de fust time, an' couldn' work as hard as de rest. Nex' mawnin' afte' dat she died. De hired man tol' de rest if dey said anything 'bout it to de marster, he'd beat dem to death, too, so ever'body kep' quiet an' de marster neber knowed.

"We worked hard in de fiel' all day, but when dark come we would all go to de Quarters an' afte' supper we would set 'roun' an' sing an' talk. Mos' of de time we had good food to eat 'cause mos' of us had our gardens, an' de Quarters cook would fix what we wanted if we brung it to her. Durin' de last years 'fo de surrender, we didn' have much to eat tho'; an' made out de best we could.

## [HW: Religion]

"De mos' fun we had was at our meetin's. We had dem mos' ever' Sunday an' dey lasted way into de night. De preacher I laked de bes' was name Mathew Ewing. He was a comely nigger, black as night, an' he sho' could read out of his han'. He neber larned no real readin' an' writin' but he sho' knowed his Bible an' would hol' his han' out an' mek lak he was readin' an' preach de purtiest preachin' you ever heered. De meetin's last frum early in de mawnin' 'til late at night. When dark come, de men folks would hang up a wash pot, bottom up'ards, in de little brush church-house us had, so's it would catch de noise an' de oberseer wouldn' hear us singin' an' shoutin'. Dey didn' min' us meetin' in de day time, but dey thought iffen we stayed up ha'f de night we wouldn' work so hard de nex' day—an' dat was de truf.

"You should'a seen some of de niggers get 'ligion. De best way was to carry 'em to de cemetery an' let 'em stand ober a grave. Dey would start singin' an' shoutin' 'bout sein' fire an' brimstone; den dey would sing some mo' an' look plum sanctified.

"When us had our big meetin's, dere would allus be some darkies frum de plantations aroun' to come. Dey would have to slip off 'cause dey marsters was afraid dey would git hitched up wid some other black boy er gal on de other plantation an' den dey would either have to buy er sell a nigger 'fo you could git any work out of him.

"We neber knowed much bout de War, 'cept dat we didn' have as much to eat er wear, an' de white men folks was all gone. Den, too, Old Miss cried a lot of de time.

**[HW: Reconstruction]**

"De Yankees come 'roun' afte' de War an' tol' us we's frea an' we shouted an' sang, an' had a big celebration fer a few days. Den we got to wonderin' 'bout what good it did us. It didn' feel no diffrunt; we all loved our marster an' missus an' stayed on wid 'em jes' lak nothin' had happened. De Yankees tried to git some of de men to vote, too, but not many did 'cause dey was scared of de

Ku Kluxers. Dey would come at night all dressed up lak ghosts an' scare us all. We didn' lak de Yankees anyway. Dey wa'nt good to us; when dey lef' we would allus sing dat leetle song what go lak dis:

**[HW: Song]**

'Old Mister Yankee, think he is so grand,
Wid his blue coat tail a draggin' on de ground!'

"I stayed on wid Old Marster afte' de surrender, wid de res', 'til I met Joshua. Joshua Young was his name an' he b'longed to de Youngs whut lived out at Waverly. I moved out dar wid him afte' we mar'ied. We didn' have no big weddin' 'cause dere wa'nt much money den. We had a preacher tho', an' den went along jes' lak we had allus been mar'ied.

"Josh, he's been daid fer a long time now but we had a good life out at Waverly an' many a night stood outside de parlor do' an' watch de white folks at dey big dances an' parties. De folks was pow'ful nice to us an' we raised a passel er chullun out dar. All of 'em 'ceptin' three be daid now. George is de oldes' of those lef'. He's a bricklayer, carpenter, preacher, an' mos anything else he 'cides to call hisse'f. He's got 19 or 20 chullun, I dis'members which. Edith ain't got so many. She live up North. I lives wid my other darter an' her gal. I named her afte' my sisters. Her name is Anna Luvenia Hulda Larissa Jane Bell Young McMillan. Dere may be more'n dat now, but anyways dere is five generations livin'.

"What I think 'bout slav'ry? Well, leetle Miss, I tell you, I wish it was back. Us was a lot better off in dem days dan we is now. If dem Yankees had lef us 'lone we'd been a lot happier. We wouldn' been on 'lief an' old age pension fer de las' three years. An' Janie May, here, I b'lieve, sure as goodness, would'a been de Missus' very smartes' gal, an' would'a stayed wid her in de Big House lak I did."

**Note:** This autobiography is exactly as related by the Negro to the field worker with exception of a few changes in spelling. Phraseology is the same.

B.Y.

## Slave Narratives

www.ingramcontent.com/pod-product-compliance
Lightning Source LLC
Chambersburg PA
CBHW061759110426
42742CB00012BB/2087